# The Cowshed

# The Cowshed
## Memories of the Chinese Cultural Revolution

Ji Xianlin

Translated from the Chinese by
**Chenxin Jiang**

Introduction by
**Zha Jianying**

WITHDRAWN

NEW YORK REVIEW BOOKS

*New York*

THIS IS A NEW YORK REVIEW BOOK
PUBLISHED BY THE NEW YORK REVIEW OF BOOKS
435 Hudson Street, New York NY 10014
www.nyrb.com

This translation was supported by a 2011 PEN Translation Fund grant.


Library of Congress Cataloging-in-Publication Data
Ji, Xianlin, author.
[Niu peng za yi. English]
The cowshed : memories of the Chinese Cultural Revolution / by Ji Xianlin ;
translated by Chenxin Jiang ; introduction by Zha Jianying.
pages cm. — (New York review books)
ISBN 978-1-59017-926-0 (alk. paper)
1. Ji, Xianlin. 2. Scholars—China—Biography. 3. China—History—
Cultural Revolution, 1966–1976—Personal narratives. 4. China—
Intellectual life—1949–1976. I. Jiang, Chenxin, translator. II. Title. III.
Title: Memories of the Chinese Cultural Revolution.
CT3990.J48A3 2015
951.05092—dc23
[B]
2015017409


ISBN 978-1-59017-926-0
Available as an electronic book; ISBN 978-1-59017-927-7

Printed in the United States of America on acid-free paper
1 3 5 7 9 10 8 6 4 2

# Contents

# Introduction

THIS MEMOIR ABOUT the Cultural Revolution by the late Chinese scholar Ji Xianlin is extraordinary, shocking, and unique. I read it many years ago when it first appeared in Chinese and shuddered at its frank, graphic depiction of the atrocities committed during that dark time. My generation of Chinese came of age during the Cultural Revolution, so the book easily rekindled some of the nightmarish memories from my own childhood in Beijing.

By now, it has been nearly forty years since the Cultural Revolution officially ended, yet in China, considering the magnitude and significance of the event, it has remained a poorly examined, under-documented subject. Official archives are off-limits. Serious books on the period, whether comprehensive histories, in-depth analyses, or detailed personal memoirs, are remarkably few. Hence the publication of *The Cowshed: Memories of the Chinese Cultural Revolution*, by an official press in Beijing, was something of an anomaly. Coming out in 1998 during a politically relaxed moment, the book probably benefited from the author's eminent status in China. A celebrated Indologist in his eighties, Ji was also a popular essayist and an avowed patriot who enjoyed good relations with the government. With genial, grandfatherly manners, he had become, in his august age, one of those avuncular figures revered by the public and loved by the media.

The book has sold well and stayed in print. But authorities also quietly took steps to restrict public discussion of the memoir, as its subject continues to be treated as sensitive. The present English edition, skillfully translated by Chenxin Jiang, is a welcome, valuable addition to the small body of work in this genre. It makes an important contribution to our understanding of that period.

Reading Ji's account again, however, has also renewed some of my old questions and frustrations. How much can we really make sense of a bizarre, unwieldy phenomenon like the Great Proletarian Cultural Revolution? Can we truly overcome barriers of limited information, fading historical memory, and persistent ideological biases to have a genuinely meaningful and illuminating conversation about it today? I wonder. The delicate circumstances surrounding Ji's memoir in China demonstrate both the entangled complexity of the events and the precarious state of historical testimony.

Like other ordinary Chinese, Ji had no idea what the Cultural Revolution was all about when Mao Zedong launched it in 1966. The son of an impoverished rural family in Shandong, Ji had managed, through diligence and scholarship, to get a solid, cosmopolitan education in republican China. Having spent a decade in Germany studying Sanskrit and other languages, Ji returned with a PhD to teach at China's preeminent Peking University where he soon became the chairman of its Eastern Languages Department. Though disliking the corrupt Chiang Kai-shek regime, he stayed away from politics, a field he'd never had any interest in. But when the communists came into power in 1949, like most educated Chinese at the time, Ji saw hope for a stronger nation and more just society.

Being a political drifter, however, was no longer an option. Under the rule of the Chinese Communist Party (CCP), mass mobilization and political campaigns became a national way of life and no one was allowed to be a bystander, least of all the intellectuals, a favorite target in Mao's periodic thought-reform campaigns.

Feeling guilty about his previous passivity, Ji eagerly reformed himself. He joined the Party in the 1950s and actively participated in the ceaseless campaigns, which had a common trait: conformity and intolerance of dissent. In the 1957 Anti-Rightist Movement, more than half a million intellectuals were denounced and persecuted, even though most of their criticisms were very mild and nearly all were Party loyalists. The fact that Ji was able to stay out of harm's way was probably due to two factors: his clean background and his good behavior. Being of poor peasant stock with no ties to the old Kuomintang regime, Ji wasn't easily labeled as a class enemy. He also came across as a rather naïve follower of political winds, one who towed the Party line sincerely, never questioned, never stuck his neck out.

In fact, he was doing just that in the first year of the Cultural Revolution. Instigated by the small ultra-leftist clique around Mao, Peking University became the first site of radicalization. The campus was quickly transformed into a chaotic zoo of factional battles, with frantic mobs rushing about attacking professors and school officials labeled as capitalist-roaders-in-power. A bewildered Ji tried his best to keep a low profile by hiding in the crowds. But he had a vulnerable spot: He abhorred a woman cadre named Nie Yuanzi, the leader of the dominant Red Guard faction on campus. Although every faction in China claimed loyalty to Chairman Mao, Nie enjoyed a special status: She penned the very first big-character poster of the Cultural Revolution, attacking certain Peking University officials and received Mao's personal endorsement for it. Disgusted by her bullying style, Ji decided, in an uncharacteristically rash moment, to join her opponents' faction. This was a fatal mistake. Nie's followers took their vengeance immediately: They raided Ji's home one night, smashing furniture and digging up, inevitably, some ridiculous evidence that Ji was a hidden counterrevolutionary.

From that moment onward, Ji's life became a dizzying descent into hell. The ensuing chapters in the book are the most shocking and painful to read. There are many searing, unforgettable vignettes. Ji's meticulous preparations for suicide, which was aborted only at the last moment by a knock on the door. The long, screaming rallies where Ji, already in his late fifties, and other victims were savagely beaten, spat on, and tortured. The betrayal by his former students and colleagues. An excruciating episode in a labor camp: Ji's body collapsed under the strain of continuous struggle sessions; his testicles became so swollen he couldn't stand up or close his legs. But the guard forced him to continue his labor, so he crawled around all day moving bricks. When he was finally allowed to visit a nearby military clinic, he had to crawl on a road for two hours to reach it, only to be refused treatment the moment the doctor learned he was a blackguard. He crawled back to the labor camp.

At the center of the book is the cowshed, the popular term for makeshift detention centers that had sprung up in many Chinese cities at the time. In Ji's case, this one was set up at the heart of the Peking University campus, where he was locked up for nine months with throngs of other fallen professors and school officials, doing manual labor and reciting tracts of Mao's writing. The inferno atmosphere of the place, the chilling variety of physical and psychological violence the guards daily inflicted on the convicts with sadistic pleasure, the starvation and human degeneration—all are vividly described. After reading the book, a Chinese intellectual friend summed it up to me: "This is our Auschwitz." Indeed, though what happened in the cowshed where Ji was held was by no means exceptional (torture and violence were widespread at the time), of all the memoirs of the Cultural Revolution I have read, I cannot think of another one that offers such a devastatingly direct and detailed testimony on the physical and mental abuse an entire imprisoned intellectual community suffered. Compared to the few other notable Chinese works in this category, such as Yang Jiang's *Ganxiao Liuji* (translated into English as *Six Chapters from My Life "Down Under"*), Ba Jin's *Sui Xiang Lu,* or Wei Junyi's *Si Tong Lu*, Ji's account has an unparalleled raw intensity. To mentally relive such darkness and to record it all in such an unswervingly candid manner could not have been easy for an elderly man: Ji was over eighty at the time of writing. In the opening chapter, he confessed to have waited for many years, in vain, for others to come forward with a testimony. Disturbed by the collective silence of the older generation and the growing ignorance of the young people about the Cultural Revolution, he finally decided to take up the pen himself.

Another noteworthy feature of the book is its entangled theme of guilt and shame. In memoirs about Maoist persecutions, authors typically portray themselves as either hapless, innocent victims or, occasionally, defiant resisters. The picture is murkier in Ji's recollection. He writes about Chinese intellectuals' eager cooperation in ideological campaigns and how, under pressure, they frequently turned on one another. He mocks his own "aptitude in crowd behavior" and admits that, until his own downfall, he had also persecuted others:

> Since we had been directed to oppose the rightists, we did. After more than a decade of continuous political struggle, the intellectuals knew the drill. We all took turns persecuting each other. This went on until the Socialist Education Movement, which, in my view, was a precursor to the Cultural Revolution.

And what was his role in the Socialist Education Movement? "Without quite knowing what I was doing, I joined the ranks of the persecutors."

But to Ji, this is a forgivable sin because if he and many other Chinese intellectuals have been guilty of persecuting one another, it was largely because the intellectuals as a class had been compelled to feel deeply guilty and shameful about themselves. Ji described how this was achieved through the fierce criticism and self-criticism sessions, a unique feature of the Maoist thought-reform campaigns. Ji's own ideological conversion was accomplished through such a ritual. Impressed by the Communist victory and early achievements, he blamed himself fervently for not being sufficiently patriotic and selfless: He was selfish to pursue his own academic studies in Germany while the Communists were fighting the Japanese invaders; he was wrong to avoid politics and to view all politics as a tainted game, because the Communist politics was genuinely idealistic and noble. Only after beating himself up about all his sins did he manage to pass the collective review and be accepted as a member of the "people." Ji describes the overwhelming sense of guilt as "almost Christian," which led to a feeling of shame and induced a powerful urge to conform and to worship the new God—the Communist Party and its Great Leader. Afterward, like a sinner given a chance to prove his worthiness, he eagerly abandoned all his previous skepticism—the trademark of a critical faculty—and became a true believer. He embraced the new cult of personality, joining others to shout at the top of his voice "Long live Chairman Mao!," as though these words were the cry of his soul.

This process, strikingly similar to religious conversion, is both revealing and characteristic. It was how, in a high-pressure, guilt-ridden atmosphere, fearful of excommunication, millions of Chinese intellectuals cast off their individuality. From there, it seems quite natural that, to prove your loyalty, you would constantly castigate yourself or any other poor sinner in the congregation suspected of impiety or treason. The feeling of guilt becomes so deeply engrained that, even after he was locked up in the cowshed, Ji racked his brain for his own faults rather than questioning the Party or the system.

Ji was obviously not a shrewd political animal or a deep thinker. Admitting that his eyes were finally opened only after the Cultural Revolution ended, he refrained from analyzing the larger political picture or interpreting the motives of those who launched the chaos. But he clearly felt that the country on the whole had failed to learn a real lesson from what happened. Toward the end of the memoir, he wrote:

> My final question is: What made the Cultural Revolution possible?
>
> This is a complicated question that I am ill-equipped to answer; the only people in a position to tackle it refuse to do so and do not seem to want anyone else to try.

Ji was of course alluding to the Chinese government's quiet ban on any deep probing of the subject, a policy still in effect today. The problem, however, is an unwieldy one without an easy solution. First and foremost is the question of Mao. Everyone knows that Mao is the chief culprit of the Cultural Revolution. Well-known historical data points to a tangle of factors behind Mao's motivation for launching it: subtle tension among the top leadership of the CCP since the Great Leap Forward, which led to a famine with an estimated thirty to forty million deaths; his desire to reassert supremacy and crush any perceived challenge to his personal power by reaching down directly to the masses; his radical, increasingly lunatic vision of permanent revolution; his deep anti-intellectualism and paranoid jealousy. The list goes on. But, from the viewpoint of the Party, allowing a full investigation and exposure of Mao's manipulations would threaten the Party's legitimacy. After all, the entire Party leadership, including those persecuted during the Cultural Revolution, had helped to create the cult of Mao and was deeply implicated in his ruthless legacy. Everyone's hands were stained with blood. If the great helmsman gets debunked, the whole ship may go down. Mao as a symbol is therefore crucial: It is tied to the survival of the Party state.

Then there is the thorny issue of the people's participation in the Cultural Revolution. The Red Guards were only the best known of the radical organizations. At the height of madness, millions of ordinary

Chinese had taken part in various forms of lawless actions and rampant violence. The estimated death toll of those who committed suicide, were tortured to death, were publically executed, or were killed in armed factional battles runs from hundreds of thousands to millions. This makes it extremely difficult, if not impossible, to bring all of the perpetrators to account.

Consequently, the situation has been handled in a manner that reflects both cynical and pragmatic calculations: After arresting and blaming it all on the ultra-leftist Gang of Four, the government officially condemned the period as a "ten-year disaster," tolerated a short period of limited public ventilation, then moved to contain the damage. It's one of those noiseless bans done through internal control; investigation, discussion, and publication have been variously forbidden, discouraged, or marginalized. Over time, the topic has faded away as though it all happened quite naturally.

This situation is of course deeply troubling. It is especially unsatisfying and unfair to those who suffered untold atrocities. Most of the teachers who were beaten up by their Red Guard students never received an apology. Most of the scholars who were tortured in the countless cowsheds continued, as Ji did, to live and work among their former persecutors. Some of these former perpetrators thrived in the new era, building successful careers and lives.

This year, as the West commemorated the seventieth anniversary of the Holocaust, I watched the media coverage while rereading Ji's memoir, and I couldn't help thinking of the remark a Chinese friend once made to me: "We are the Jews in this country." His whole family had suffered very badly during the Cultural Revolution and they still live in Beijing today, among those who had once persecuted them. The analogy between the Holocaust and the Cultural Revolution is of course a stretched one, yet it makes one wonder about an impossible scenario: If Hitler's portrait was still hanging in the main square of Berlin today, if the Nazi Party continued to rule, albeit with different policies, and if the Jews still had to live in Germany, surrounded by former tormentors and a population complicit in the crime who were never punished nor publicly repented, how would they feel?

That's contemporary China, where history is a messy unfinished business, the people are accustomed to internalized trauma, and society cheerfully marches on with its skeletons in the closet and ghosts weeping in the air. It is a place where the victimized individual and community are often expected to get over it and move on. You keep quiet or you are muzzled—either way it is for the collective good, the national harmony. A rising great nation, in short, cannot let memories of past wrongs poison the present or the future.

Proud of his patriotism, Ji also liked to discuss China's bright future. His reputation grew rather mixed among liberal intellectuals in his late years because, with his rosy-eyed pronouncements about Chinese civilization's inevitable leadership in the twenty-first century, he often sounded like a cultural nationalist. But when it came to the Cultural Revolution, Ji drew the line: He just couldn't accept that it was being deliberately expunged from the collective memory. There was simmering resentment, he insisted, among a lot of older Chinese intellectuals around him, who have had no recourse for their past suffering. And this was not good, in his opinion, for building a true socialist nation.

But Ji also worried about "stepping on people's toes." After writing the first draft in 1988, he kept his memoir in a drawer for years, for fear it might be viewed as a personal vendetta. He then revised it heavily, toning down the prose and keeping most of the persecutors unnamed. He says he wants no revenge, just to write a honest historical document, so that young Chinese would know the past and would not let it happen again. He sounded apologetic about letting his emotions get the better of him in the earlier draft. Still, the reader can probably catch a strange tone of sarcasm and self-mockery in the narrator's voice. I found Ji's tone odd and puzzling at first until it occurred to me that this is not an uncommon rhetorical device in Chinese writing or talking: To control seething anger or to deflect unbearable pain, one often turns to black humor or sarcastic hyperbole. A Chinese elementary-school teacher who was tortured and jeered at in public struggle sessions during the Cultural Revolution told me that the sense of physical and psychological violation was so ferocious it felt like being gang-raped. He had nightmares about it for years. Later, a friend pointed out that he would adopt a facetious tone whenever he spoke about the experience. "I hadn't noticed the tone myself," he told me. "I think I turned it all into a joke because I can't bear the pain and the shame with a straight face."

Ji also seemed to suffer survivor's shame. Even though his career flourished after the Cultural Revolution, he repeatedly mentioned his ambivalence about his failed attempt at suicide. This has to do with an ancient code of honor for a Confucian scholar. In the memoir, Ji recalls his first encounter after the Cultural Revolution with the senior apparatchik Zhou Yang. Zhou had supervised the persecution of many intellectuals until he himself was persecuted during the Cultural Revolution. Zhou's first words to Ji were: "It used to be said that 'the scholar can be killed, but he cannot be humiliated.' But the Cultural Revolution proved that not only can the scholar be killed, he can also be humiliated." Zhou roared with laughter, but Ji knew it was a bitter laugh. Many scholars and writers committed suicide in the early part of the Cultural Revolution to avoid the indignities they faced. To Ji and perhaps many others, to have endured unspeakable debasement and humiliation, and survived, somehow reflects a weakness in one's moral character and is therefore a continuous source of shame. Ironically, all those decades of Maoist thought-reform campaigns have failed to destroy this Confucian pride of a scholar which, sadly, became either his last defense of honor or source of shame.

Ji Xianlin died in Beijing in 2009. In a final set of interviews conducted from his hospital room, the ninety-seven-year-old scholar was still talking about the need to remember the Cultural Revolution, still convinced that one day China would be ready for a real national introspection about it. The two people he admired the most in his life, he said, were the Confucian scholar Liang Shuming and the People's Liberation Army general Peng Dehuai, because they had "backbones" and dared to speak truth to the emperor. Liang and Peng are known to be the only two Chinese individuals who criticized Mao in person. For his contribution to the field of Indology, Ji was honored by the governments of China and India. His work as a linguist and a paleographer are highly specialized. But among the reading public in China, he will most likely be remembered for *The Cowshed*, the powerful and important personal testimony about the darkest moment in modern Chinese history.

—ZHA JIANYING

POSTSCRIPT

Two years after Ji Xianlin's death, a Peking University alumna named Zhang Manling who had been close to Ji published a piece about their friendship and made a few unusual revelations. In 1989, after the students began their hunger strike on Tiananmen Square, Ji and several other Peking University professors decided to publicly show their solidarity with the youngsters by paying them a visit. Ji, the oldest and most famous of the professors, traveled in high style: Sitting on a stool on top of a flat-backed tricycle, which was fastened with a tall white banner that said "Rank One Professor Ji Xianlin," the seventy-eight-year-old Ji was peddled by a student from the west-side campus across the city. When they finally arrived in Tiananmen Square, the students burst into delighted cheers. During the post-massacre purge, at all the faculty meetings where everyone was forced to *biao tai* (declare their position), Ji would only say, "Don't ask me, or I'll say it was a patriotic democratic movement." Then one day, Ji walked off from his campus residence, hailed a taxi, and asked to be taken to the local public security bureau. "I'm Professor Ji Xianlin of Peking University," Ji said to the police on arrival. "I visited Tiananmen Square twice. I stirred up the students, so please lock me up together with them. I'm over seventy, and I don't want to live anymore." The policemen were so startled they called Peking University officials, who rushed over and forcibly brought Ji back to campus.

It was, again, one of those high-pressured, terrifying, and tragic moments in China's long history. But this time, acting alone, Ji lived up to the honor of a true Confucius scholar.

# Translator's Note

THE GREAT PROLETARIAT Cultural Revolution was launched by Mao Zedong in 1966 to root out class enemies from within the Party. Cowsheds were improvised prisons built during this time on Chinese university campuses to house intellectuals who were considered class enemies. The cowshed derived its unusual name from its prisoners, known as "cow devils." The prisons were run by the paramilitary student organizations that styled themselves as Red Guards, and most existed only in the early stages of the movement, from around 1966 to 1969. In this memoir, written and published some three decades after the events it describes, Ji Xianlin recalls being targeted as a class enemy and struggled against, in the parlance of the time. A prominent scholar of Sanskrit and Pali, he was eventually imprisoned in the cowshed at Peking University, where he resumed teaching after his release.

# Author's Preface

GIVEN THAT THIS book was written six years ago, the gentle reader may be wondering why it is only being published now, in 1998. That's odd, you're thinking. There must be a story behind this delay. And there is. I make no secret of my private reasons for delaying the publication of this book. During the Cultural Revolution, I was struggled against and stepped on by Red Guards, and it looked as though I would never be rehabilitated. But when I was rehabilitated, and my academic and political careers took off, some of the guards who had tortured me may have feared for themselves now that I was in a position to take revenge.

But I never did. This isn't because I am a forgiving person—I love, hate, envy, and crave revenge just like anyone else. But whenever I am tempted to get even with my persecutors, I think back to the atmosphere on campus during the Cultural Revolution, when anyone who joined a faction seemed to have drunk a personality-altering potion that alienated them from their own humanity and made them nonhuman. I say nonhuman because calling human beings brutes is an insult to the animals. Animals eat people because they are hungry. Unlike human beings, animals don't tell lies, they have no wiles, and they don't make rambling speeches full of classical allusions to why someone deserves to be eaten before opening their mouths to gobble him up.[1] So I am calling these individuals nonhumans instead of brutes. I know that I myself never stopped believing in the Cultural Revolution, even as I was being persecuted. Many of the persecutors were also victims of the revolution, just like the persecuted; the two simply happened to find themselves in different positions, which is why I could not find it in myself to take revenge on my persecutors.

That was one reason why I refrained from publishing this book; but I also had other private concerns.

Anyone who knows anything about the Cultural Revolution knows that just about every school, government institution, factory, production unit, and even some army divisions at the time were divided into opposing factions. Each of the two factions considered itself to be truly leftist and truly revolutionary, whereas its opponents were not. In fact, neither was superior to the other—they both beat up their victims, stole and destroyed things, and murdered innocent people. There is no point discussing which of them was right. Yet the invisible, irrational partisan emotions of the times caused great division. Even within families, it tore marriages apart and caused children to denounce their parents. In eighty years of reading widely, I've never come across another social movement that took such a strong psychological hold on its participants. The phenomenon deserves to be studied carefully by sociologists and psychologists.

I, too, was an enthusiastic member of one faction and extremely partisan. But unlike many others, I nearly paid for my partisanship with my life. As the head of my department, I couldn't join the masses in "making revolution." In fact, as I listened to their chants of "There is no crime in revolution, it is reasonable to revolt," I realized that I myself risked becoming a target of their revolt. But I had never taken an interest in politics, and before 1949 I had not been associated with the Kuomintang at all. So although I couldn't avoid being labeled a "capitalist-roader" and "counterrevolutionary academic authority," after the first two waves of persecution had passed, no one accused me of major crimes, and I was considered one of the masses like everyone else.

If I had kept my head down, I could easily have remained neutral and stayed out of trouble for the next few years. Depending on how you look at it, either I had the misfortune of being too stubborn or stubbornness was my one saving grace. I watched the Empress Dowager terrorize the campus, bully the faction opposed to her, cut off their water and electricity, and even look the other way when her Red Guards caused the death of a student.[2] As Confucius put it, "If even this can be tolerated, what then is considered intolerable?" I decided to join the weaker of the two factions, the one opposed to Nie Yuanzi. She had a well-deserved reputation for vindictiveness; this book chronicles what happened to me as a result.

When I joined a faction, partisan feeling gripped me like a python and would not let go. I remember doing and saying all kinds of irrational things. Partisanship fizzled out at the end of the Cultural Revolution, but people still remembered which side they used to be on. Many of my colleagues were members of the opposing faction, people who struggled against me, interrogated me, and beat me up. Many of them seem to regret what happened. No one is perfect, and I consider them good comrades who made a few horrific mistakes under the spell of partisanship. But if they were to discover this manuscript in my drawer, they would be convinced that I was plotting to exact my revenge. Even though I hadn't included their names, they would all recognize themselves instantly, and it would become virtually impossible for us to keep working together. To avoid the awkwardness that would inevitably ensue, I refrained from publishing this book long after having completed it.

Then why did you write this book in the first place? the reader may wonder. It is a fair question.

I originally had no plans to write a book about the Cultural Revolution, which explains why this book was not written until sixteen years after the Cultural Revolution ended in 1976. During these sixteen years, I reflected, observed, puzzled, debated with myself, and waited. I regretted having been so politically naïve as to have supported the Cultural Revolution until the Gang of Four was toppled in 1976. To this date, no one has been able to explain what caused the Cultural Revolution, a brutal disaster that drove China to the brink of economic collapse, but many other people recognized it for the disaster that it was long before I did. I was deeply ashamed of having been so naïve.

Once I began to reflect on the Cultural Revolution, I realized that the perpetrators were not addressing it in the right way. It's true that we shouldn't dwell on the past, but in this case we haven't reflected sufficiently on it. As I have mentioned, most people were deceived at the time, but even those who were deceived should seize this unparalleled opportunity to reflect on just how they were taken in, to avoid making the same mistake again. As for the others, there were some truly wicked people among the perpetrators, whom we used to call chameleons. They were masters at seeing which way the political winds were blowing. As soon as the winds changed, they would change their tune. Some of them would later pretend to be upstanding citizens, some would marry generals and cadres whom they could rely on for political protection, and some would bide their time, waiting for the right opportunity to make a grab for power again. These people are ambitious, skilled flatterers who have countless tricks up their sleeves. They are the cancer cells of our socialist society, and letting them off the hook for their crimes was a mistake. Chinese society today appears peaceful and harmonious, and things seem to be going well. But our society is ethically hollow, local government is often corrupt, and many individuals are incompetent. If we trace these problems to their roots, we are likely to find them in the Cultural Revolution and in the people mentioned above.

These conclusions are the results of my reflection and observation, the things that trouble me. I hoped that someone would record their own experience of this disaster. All kinds of people, including respected generals who had risked their lives defending the people, Party leaders who had sacrificed everything for the revolutionary cause, as well as many loyal and hardworking intellectuals, authors, and actors, were publicly humiliated and persecuted. It was said of the ancient emperors, "When the bird has been shot down, the bow is put away; when the hare is dead, the hunting dog is killed and boiled." Our socialist fatherland had perpetrated outrages of which even the ancient emperors would have been ashamed. I was sure that one of the victims would channel his indignation into an account of his experiences. But I waited days, months, years, and still no one ventured to write about their anguish, or even dictate an account to someone else. I was disappointed and deeply concerned. If no one wrote about this disaster, our children's children wouldn't learn from our mistakes, and the next time a similar situation arose, someone else would do something equally stupid and brutal. The thought terrifies me. If you tell today's young people about the Cultural Revolution, they stare at you wide-eyed, as though they think you're lying. A few years ago, a certain form of scar literature emerged, but as far as I am concerned, the young authors of those books weren't scarred by the Cultural Revolution: at most, they had minor scrapes that needed a little disinfectant and a bandage.[3] Those who had been truly scarred had buried their experiences deep within themselves and were refusing to talk about them. I was waiting for a victim of the Cultural Revolution who would be willing to talk about his scars.

I have another wish that is unlikely ever to be fulfilled. While I've long hoped for the persecuted to tell their story, I believe that one of the persecutors should also come forward and tell their story—the story of what drove them to take such pleasure in hurting others. Most of the Red Guards are now middle-aged, and some of them have done very well for themselves. Even if they have never been held accountable for their crimes, how can they live with the knowledge of what they did? There are scores of former Red Guards, and if one of them were to write about his or her experience, the persecutor's account could be read alongside that of the persecuted. That, too, would be an incalculable service to our people. I am not demanding that the writer wallow in guilt and self-incrimination, but simply suggesting that he or she offer an objective description of what happened. Surely such an account would earn praise rather than blame for its writer.

So I have waited twelve years for accounts of the Cultural Revolution from both the perpetrators and the victims. I've waited all night until daybreak, and yet my hopes have not been fulfilled. By the time I wrote this book in 1992, many of the generation who were persecuted were beginning to pass away, as was only natural, since they had grown old. As our ancestors said, "You could grow old waiting for the Yellow River to become clear." I couldn't do anything about one of the books I was hoping for, but as for the other: after all, I was a victim of the Cultural Revolution, and as opposed to waiting for someone to write the book I wanted to read, I thought I might as well roll up my sleeves and write it myself. That is how *The Cowshed* came to be. I have never told a lie in print, and now I am setting out what happened exactly as it was. But now that I've written this book, I haven't given up on the other books I still hope one day to read. I am writing this preface partly in hopefulness that those other books will be written.

—JI XIANLIN
*Beijing, March 9, 1998*

# INTRODUCTION

EVERYONE IN CHINA knew what the cowshed was, but no one knew its official name. We have come to value the rule of law, which requires things to be given their proper names. But how could a lawful name have been found for the cowshed, the very existence of which showed that the rule of law had broken down?

The term "cowshed" wasn't used much at Peking University. The authorities referred to the makeshift prisons in which professors were imprisoned on their own college campuses as *laogai,* or reform through labor camps. Later people started calling them blackguard camps, and the name caught on. Blackguards, as the name implies, specialize in doing bad things and giving the Red Guards a hard time, so the place where they were locked up was nicknamed the blackguard camp.

I had the good fortune not only to have seen a cowshed—or rather, to have been forced to see it—but to have lived in one for about nine months. It was no life of luxury, but I did gain a rare opportunity to witness the Cultural Revolution from the inside. The heavens were kind to me: Another such opportunity would be harder to find than the proverbial needle in a haystack. Not only was I born in interesting times but I ended up in the most interesting of places, the cowshed, in the thick of the action. Would anyone these days build a prison for me and ensure its security by guarding it day and night?

I study Buddhist history and precepts, but I've always been most intrigued by Buddhist superstitions, especially those concerning hell. These folk beliefs occasionally surface in canonical texts, but they truly come alive in oral tradition, in which centuries of torture inflicted upon ordinary folk by ancient Chinese and Indian regimes have been refined into a masterpiece of sadism guaranteed to make the listener's hair stand on end.

Decades of studying an assortment of Eastern and Western hells have led me to the conclusion that the Western hell is far too simple, naïve, tame. Take Dante's *Inferno*: His poetry may be sublime, but the hell he describes is superficial, unimaginative, comical. It has none of the depths of India's hells, which, amplified by wicked Chinese embellishments, are a veritable pagoda of horrors. Books like the *Jade Record*—a Chinese tract about hell illustrated with lakes of fire and mountains of knives, saws, vats of oil, bull- and horse-headed devils, villains, and props—dazzle the beholder and can only inspire awe. They prove the folk wisdom of the East to be superior to the erudition of Western civilization.

I thought the imaginative powers of these anonymous storytellers unsurpassable until my time in the cowshed forced me to concede that the Red Guards' inventions far outstripped those of all their predecessors. The administration of the actual cowshed outdid that of the storied hell of ancient India. Dante himself would've learned a lot from these literary masterpieces.

My guess is that some of the students who became Red Guards used to attend my lectures on Buddhism. They may not have learned all that much about Buddhist history or beliefs, but they must have paid close attention to the Buddhist hell, because they managed to put theory into practice by building a cowshed in Beijing that was the envy of the land and widely emulated. Their success underscores how the student can indeed surpass the teacher, proving that the decades I spent teaching at Peking University were not in vain. As one of their victims, I have nothing but admiration for all of them.

In fact, my students improvised ingeniously on what they had gleaned from their studies. Without having to build mountains of knives or fill vats with boiling oil, without any demonic aid, the Red Guards created an atmosphere of terror that far outstripped that of Buddhist creations. In the Narakas (the Buddhist hell), devils follow the orders of Yanluo, the ruler and judge of the underworld, and spear their victims, hurling them into the oil. But such physical torment cannot compare with the psychological cruelty practiced by the Red Guards in the name of combating revisionism. For instance, at Peking University, the Red Guards forced their charges to learn quotations from Chairman Mao by heart. Buddhist devils don't force their prisoners to memorize sutras and chant them, punishing every mistake with a slap to the face. Their victims don't suffer through the daily lectures I remember so well: inmates assembled in rows each evening at dusk, the barking of guards, the sounds of beatings echoing in the clear night sky. Shadows flickered in the thin darkness by a hill outside the compound. To my dismay, I could sometimes make out—from the corner of my eye—the few free citizens who had stopped by to admire the spectacle.

Indeed, the cowshed was a hub of new inventions, which made life for its inmates both exciting and terrifying. Our senses were sharpened to the point of paranoia. Never before had I experienced such a state of constant anxiety, and no outsider could possibly understand what it was like. Even though tens of thousands of people were incarcerated in the cowshed—no one knows exactly how many there were —they represented only a tiny fraction of China's vast population. As I have said, this was a rare opportunity. Aren't writers always advised to live life before writing about it? Of course, hardly anyone would volunteer to be imprisoned in the cowshed, and a willing victim wouldn't necessarily have met the strict entrance criteria.

As one of the happy few inmates of the cowshed, I almost paid for my good fortune with my life. Since then, I have felt that someone should write about what it was like. I suppose I could have done so myself: I am no writer, but I am a bit of a scribbler. Although I was unwilling to dredge up painful memories of that time, I hoped that another writer who had done time in the cowshed would record that terrible history. It would be a tremendous service to readers in China and beyond.

But I waited and waited. I devoured all the books and articles I could find on the subject, but never found what I was hoping for. Gifted writers among the survivors of the cowshed must number in the thousands. Why this silence? There is no time to lose: As each generation of survivors ages, these fleeting memories will be lost for good. That would be an immeasurable loss.

In 1992, not twenty years after the Cultural Revolution, people have already begun to forget what happened. When I tell young people about what happened to me, they stare back at me, their faces clouded with disbelief. (Sometimes even middle-aged people stare too.) He must be exaggerating, they think, he must have some ulterior motive—that can't really have happened. Although they are too polite to contradict me, I can read the incredulity in their eyes, and it distresses me.

I mourn, because although I escaped with my life, no one understands my experience. Even to family or close friends, I've only revealed bits and pieces of what happened, most I've kept to myself to this day. I anticipate that my listeners will sympathize, and I mourn because they do not. The older I grow, the more alone I become. My elders grow frail like leaves in late autumn; young people are alien to me. Will my secrets die with me? The mere thought reminds me how

4

alone I am. I fear that if society learns nothing from the collective experience of tens of thousands like me, we will have suffered in vain. And yet, setting these fears aside, I am convinced that an honest account of this period would be useful to all nations, if only as an example of what not to do and what to do. No ill can come of it.

After thinking long and hard, I've decided to take up the task myself. My account will contain no shade of untruth or exaggeration. I will not stoop to sensationalism. Rather, I will record events just as they happened, without adding or subtracting anything. I've never paid heed to idle criticism. The talent of lying to win favor is one that I neither possess nor desire. I am confident that my memory holds true. Now that I've been baptized by the fires of the Cultural Revolution hell, I fear nothing, as running water cannot intimidate one who has crossed oceans. If any of my readers wish to read themselves into portraits of certain individuals, to treat the scars pointed to in these accounts as their own, I can only say: Be my guest. My account may not be literary, but it has been traded for blood and tears. I think my readers will understand that this book is not a novel.

# THE SOCIALIST EDUCATION MOVEMENT

IN THE EARLY sixties, a socialist education campaign that emphasized class struggle swept through China, throwing Peking University into chaos. The rules of political infighting were the same as they'd always been: If you get me this time, I'll make sure to get you back next time. Eventually, the crossfire died down, and we were all sent to the villages to be reeducated by peasants.

Not long after the International Hotel Conference in the autumn of 1965, I was posted to Nankou Village just outside Beijing to help lead a team of students working there as part of the Socialist Education Movement.[1] As the assistant leader of the group, I was responsible for Party discipline in the Peking University contingent. Nankou was a small village by the mountain pass, and before the railways were built, it had been a bustling market town. The elderly people in the village told me that the streets used to be full of shops, the hotels rowdy with men playing dice all night, hundreds of camels lying in the streets each night. There was nothing left of that time but crumbling edifices and old people's memories.

The impetus for the Cultural Revolution came from the very top. In November 1965, the literary critic Yao Wenyuan wrote an essay called "On the New Historical Play *Hai Rui Dismissed from Office*."[2] It was a tendentious reading of Wu Han's play that had no basis in fact, but Yao was a mere puppet saying exactly what the Party leaders wanted him to say. At the time, I was still in Nankou. I remember reading the essay and dismissing it as an incompetent piece of work. I didn't have a political cell in my brain, so although we had been learning about class struggle and talking politics every day since Liberation, I couldn't see that the essay was actually all about class struggle and would set off a violent political storm.[3] One of my faults is that I have never been able to keep my opinions to myself, so I told anyone who would listen what I thought of the piece. I pointed out that the play had nothing to do with Peng Dehuai. I even said openly that I knew all three co-authors of the controversial column "Notes from a Three-Family Village," and that one of them was a good friend.[4] Wu Han, the historian and deputy major of Beijing, had been a classmate of mine at Tsinghua in the 1930s. When I returned to Beijing in 1946, he had asked me to speak to his students at Tsinghua University, and invited me to his home. It never occurred to me that some of my listeners would later seize on my words to attack me. One of the students at Nankou was a young man from a good class background, the son of a revolutionary martyr, who was always very respectful to me. I had mentally designated him my successor, the student who would take over my work. Instead, it turned out that this man with a smile on his face was taking note of everything I said, and would later dredge up all my comments to label me a "hanger-on of the Three-Family Village." Incidentally, he has since abandoned his rightful place in the vanguard of the proletariat and slipped away to live in a small European country.

Yao's warped use of so-called evidence to accuse his victims of nameless crimes set a dangerous precedent, and would be copied by countless others in the Cultural Revolution. He may only have been mimicking a technique practiced by Party leaders, but his influence corrupted the thinking of a generation of young people, and its after-effects continue to this day.

One incident made a deep impression on me. Our work unit in Nankou Village included teams from the Central Broadcasting Station as well as the police, or Public Security Bureau. There were no uniforms, and we were under orders never to discuss our work. Our motley crew got on extraordinarily well. I befriended a young police officer called Chen, who had spent ten years serving on the police force. He was extremely easygoing, and we could talk about anything. I noticed that he always burned his letters after reading them, whereas I was in the habit of keeping all correspondence and receipts, regardless of whether they served an obvious purpose. Chen would destroy everything, even something as trivial as one of the official greeting cards the Public Security Bureau sent to every policeman. One day, I couldn't resist asking him, "Why do you burn all your letters?"

"To make sure there's no trace left of them."

"Couldn't you just tear them up and toss them in the latrines?"

"They might still be recoverable."

"You're being too paranoid."

"In our line of work, we can never forget that if you get in trouble once you'll never hear the end of it."

I was stunned. I had never thought that way. I certainly knew I possessed enough flaws for someone to criticize if they wanted to denounce me. But as I hadn't opposed the Party, or socialism, or joined a counterrevolutionary organization, I figured I couldn't be labeled a counterrevolutionary. Later events proved Chen right. Before long, I would get in serious trouble for opposing the influential Nie Yuanzi. "In twenty years of teaching, I earned myself / Nothing but a counterrevolutionary label," I once wrote. But that is another story.

# JUNE FOURTH, 1966

NANKOU MAY HAVE been in the middle of nowhere, but it wasn't completely isolated from the world of politics—after all, we had been sent there in the name of class struggle. And although I disagreed with the leftists who ate and breathed and talked of nothing but class struggle, even I could see that in a place like Nankou, some changes were needed. But I had no idea of the bigger storm brewing. At the center of the storm was Beijing, and at the center of Beijing was Peking University.

From Nankou, this all seemed very far away. At first it appeared to have nothing to do with us. We felt closer to the rhythm of the seasons than we did to events in the capital. Spring often comes late to mountain villages. But the almond and peach and pear trees eventually bloomed, carpeting the mountainsides in pink and white blossoms. The news that filtered through to the village suggested that another political movement was looming. Even from our peaceful village, far from campus, we could sense the turmoil on the horizon.

With May came more troubling news from Beijing. The politburo released a flurry of documents, including the May 16th Notification that officially launched the Great Proletariat Cultural Revolution.[1] Politics didn't interest me in the least, and I was living my life in Nankou, oblivious to how these developments might affect me. In the meantime, the mood on campus had shifted. Colleagues who had been back to Beijing told us that the constant squabbling between factions had escalated into violence. A high-ranking government official spent several evenings meeting with university students, hoping to calm things down, but the effects of this attempt were short-lived. On May 25, Nie Yuanzi and her followers in the Philosophy Department put up a big-character poster attacking key members of the Peking University Party Committee and Beijing Municipal Party Committee. It was entitled: "What Are Song Shuo, Lu Ping, and Peng Peiyun Really Doing in the Cultural Revolution?" Big-character posters, the handwritten posters put up in public places to denounce "counterrevolutionary" people and institutions, were going to become extremely popular, and this one touched off a huge debate right away. Students from both factions huddled in large groups outside the cafeteria and argued late into the night. In fact, no one could keep track of how many factions there were and how many students were involved. Now that the crowds had been stirred up, there was no stopping them.

None of us in Nankou knew what the big-character poster said. But we could tell that this would only intensify the Socialist Education Movement. The International Hotel Conference had been a setback for the camp opposing Lu Ping, the erstwhile president of the university and Party Committee secretary, and it was their turn to take revenge.

On June 1st, the Central Broadcasting Station unexpectedly broadcast the text of the big-character poster and quoted Mao commending it as a "Marxist-Leninist poster." I didn't know what a Marxist-Leninist poster was back then and still don't. In Nankou, we talked about the broadcast, but it wasn't a heated discussion, and our disagreements didn't divide us into factions. The campus news we occasionally received was like distant thunder on a cloudless day.

Since we had no real sense of what was happening, we seldom gave it any thought. We were happy to go on being educated by the peasants.

In Nankou were about eight of us from the Eastern Languages Department. This included both the Party secretary and myself, the department head. According to the new rules, both of us were, by definition, "in power," and hence to be punished as capitalist-roaders. In Nankou, the capitalist-roaders got on well with all the other teachers and students. We trundled on happily without realizing how dangerously close we were to the cliff's edge, while those ready to shove us over wagged their tails respectfully like so many pet pugs.

On June fourth, the Party secretary and I received a sudden order to return to campus to join the revolution. The order was unanticipated, though perhaps if we had been more politically aware we would've expected it. Having brought no books nor any other possessions save a few blankets and washbasins, we packed our bags immediately and piled into the van the university had sent to pick us up. Of course we were a little nostalgic to be leaving Nankou, which had been our home for the past seven or eight months. I was reminded of a poem: "When the traveler looks back at the trees of where he once lodged, the place begins to look like home."[2] There was revolution in the air. The Party branch secretary said nothing. He had more of a nose for politics and more experience of class struggle than I did, so perhaps he could anticipate the welcome that awaited us. Neither of us knew his fate. Even I was a little unsettled at having to leave so abruptly. I used to eagerly anticipate visits to Beijing, but this time returning to Yanyuan—"the garden of Yan," the familiar Peking University campus—felt like a step into the unknown.

Less than two hours later, we were back in Beijing. I had been expecting the department to welcome us warmly, given that we were the Party branch secretary and department head, but no one came to greet us. Our first glimpse of the campus shocked us. There were cars parked everywhere, to say nothing of the sea of bicycles outside buildings and on lawns, taking up every available inch of space. The grounds swarmed with students and visitors, and just past the campus gates, our car slowed to a halt because of the crowds. Needless to say, there was no special homecoming for us.

We were told that the university had been in this state of chaos since June 1st, thronging with people who had come to see the first Marxist-Leninist big-character poster. To them, Peking University was a Jerusalem, Leiyin Temple, or Mecca, a holy ground that cleansed pilgrims from all evil. Tens of thousands of students arrived each day, initially from all over Beijing and then from schools across the country. Beijingers naturally wanted a share of the action. They swarmed onto the campus and melted into the crowds of students who were raising havoc. There were big-character posters everywhere, pinned on walls, pasted on trees or on sidewalks, all declaring their full support of the first Marxist-Leninist poster.

As I got out of the car, I looked at the commotion around me in amazement. No one was there to welcome me, but no one was there to struggle against me either. I was a free man for now. The Party branch secretary wasn't so lucky. He had been designated a capitalist-roader, and Red Guards arrested him the moment we reached campus. We wouldn't see each other again for several years. The big-character posters accused him of all kinds of crimes: They called him the "Shepherd Secretary," a member of the "Lu Ping gang," a reactionary. Lu Ping himself was in even deeper trouble. The university president had been a leader of the 1935 anti-Japanese student protests and once served as the deputy minister of railways. As a result of having been named in the first Marxist-Leninist poster, he was now the crowd's principal target, and I heard that he was being struggled against day and night. Most of the struggle sessions took place outside his living quarters on campus. He was forced to stand on a low wall while the crowds chanted slogans and their leaders accused him of all kinds of crimes. Lu Ping's quarters became a minor campus attraction: Every passerby had the right to pluck him from his private residence and struggle against him, like a crowd paying to see a star performer at the Peking opera of prerevolutionary times.

Although no one had come to arrest me yet, and I was allowed to live at home and move about freely, I could tell I was in a precarious position. I read a few of the big-character posters attacking me. One day, at Block 40, the dorm that housed students from my department, I read a poster criticizing an essay of mine called "Springtime in Yanyuan." The Red Guards claimed that springtime represented capitalism, and celebrating the spring amounted to celebrating capitalism. I was bewildered. If anything, spring has always been the sign of new life—since when had it been appropriated as the emblem of capitalism? Then again, Yao's essay espoused just this sort of crooked logic, as did later essays criticizing the authors of the "Three-Family Village" column. Yao's methods had the seal of official approval, and everyone imitated them. Theories of "narrative as a counterrevolutionary tool" abounded, and soon enough everyone was an expert in these methods. At that point, I was still a true believer. But I knew perfectly well that the springtime I wrote about had nothing to do with capitalism and everything to do with the change of seasons. As I read the poster about my essay, I couldn't help snorting audibly. The enemy's eyes and ears were everywhere; like my heedless comments on Yao's essay, this single snort would later be used against me.

For now, I was free to explore the bustling campus, which was even more crowded than it had been the day we returned. For many students from distant provinces who had never been to Beijing, this was a perfect opportunity to see the capital. Yanyuan, which used to be so spacious and peaceful, began to feel suffocating. There were people everywhere. I felt tiny, like a kernel of rice in a granary.

As far as I could make out, this phase of the revolution was directed at the capitalist-roaders. Anyone in a position of authority was designated a capitalist-roader, from the central government to the lowliest administrative office. That meant there were capitalist-roaders everywhere, and their attackers were everywhere too. Even though I supported the revolution, I did wonder how every single department happened to have a capitalist-roader. And if all our leaders were capitalist saboteurs, how had we achieved anything at all? Discussing these doubts with anyone was out of the question. The "direction of the revolution" had been laid down by the authorities and the Red Guards, and like everyone else, I had learned that revolution was not a dinner party. We had spent years studying the dialectic method and being told that materialists had to seek truth from facts. What did denouncing capitalist-roaders have to do with truth or facts? The whole thing baffled me.

The Red Guards grew creative. Among other things, they invented the practice of hanging large wooden placards around the necks of all the capitalist-roaders at Peking University. Since Peking University was now the capital of Cultural Revolution fashion, the use of these placards spread rapidly. Although I never observed it at our school, they were used elsewhere as a form of torture: The placards were made heavier and the steel wire suspending them thinner so that it would cut into the flesh of their victims. I witnessed countless struggle sessions. If the session was held indoors, the capitalist-roaders would stand onstage with their heads bowed, wearing their placards, while the "revolutionary masses" sat on chairs; outdoors, they would be made to stand somewhere where the crowds could see them, on a rock, a low stone wall, or a chair. There was no formal order of proceedings, but the sessions always took place in the same way. Someone would read from Mao's sayings, and then the leader would call for ——, the capitalist-roader, to be brought to the front. The unfortunate individual would have his arms twisted behind his back with two Red Guards pushing down on his head as they led him onto the podium. Then the crowds would go wild shouting slogans: "Long live Chairman Mao!" Someone would make a speech, and whatever was said was by default true. All the capitalist-roaders had committed the same crimes: They opposed the Party, socialism, and the Great Leader. The masses could pin any label they liked on their unfortunate victims. They would always ask the capitalist-roader whether he admitted his guilt. If he hesitated, they would beat him savagely. It was unclear what the struggle sessions achieved, except to torment their victims. Some in the audience were completely earnest, others found it good fun, and still others took sadistic pleasure in the torture. Whatever the case, they all enjoyed themselves, and visitors from other provinces took what they had observed back to their hometowns, so that the practice of holding struggle sessions quickly spread beyond Peking University. The airplane position had not been invented yet.[3] It may not even have been invented in Yanyuan; to this day, no one has come forward to patent it.

Within my department, the Party branch secretary and the elderly professor N. were the main targets of big-character posters and struggle sessions: the former was, as we have said, a capitalist-roader, and the latter had conveniently been labeled a "counterrevolutionary academic authority" and "historical reactionary." The struggle sessions were brutal. I only saw one involving the Party branch secretary, which took place in front of a makeshift stand that had been built as a board for big-character posters. The posters all referred to him as the Shepherd Secretary and listed his supposed crimes. He stood bent over at the waist. Instead of a wooden placard, there was a piece of paper pasted onto his shirt. It bore his name, crossed out with a big red X. This was a trick borrowed from the courts, which had in turn taken them from Qing dynasty novels that depicted criminals led to the executioner's block wearing large wooden placards that bore their name and a red cross. Now the Party branch secretary was the criminal. There was much chanting of slogans. Eventually, a big-character poster was pasted onto his back. He was ordered to make his way home and forbidden to tear the poster off before he got there.

The first struggle session against my colleague N. was in the large conference room in the Foreign Languages Building. The corridors were plastered with caricatures that depicted him as a spear-wielding devil with blood dripping from his teeth. Inside the conference room, the mob directed its own bloodthirsty frenzy at a helpless old man who wasn't allowed to speak. Spit flew, as did false accusations. Someone put a wastepaper basket on his head. A Red Guard splashed a full bottle of blue ink down his shirt, making it look like a military camouflage shirt. Eventually he was ordered to go home.

It was decided that a large-scale struggle session would take place on June 18th, on a high podium next to Block 29 in the student dorms. An instinct for self-preservation told me to stay away. I sat at home, listening to the distant chanting of slogans. Later I was told that anyone who had been denounced as a capitalist-roader up until then was hauled onto the podium and harangued. Then all the capitalist devils were unceremoniously kicked off the stage and left to pick themselves up out of the mud and limp home. Even the elderly and infirm were hoisted up to the podium in large wicker baskets, kicked off the stage, and carried back to their sickbeds in baskets. That night, students rampaged around campus beating people up and screaming at them, not seeing that they resembled devils more than their victims did.

From then on, every June 18th would be set aside for struggling against counterrevolutionary devils. Only two years later, I would find myself onstage too.

# CHOOSING A LABEL THAT FIT

I WAS LUCKY to be free. But I was also uneasy because I knew that I would eventually end up with a political label or "hat," as people called them at the time. I had headed the Eastern Languages Department for twenty years, and the mob was unlikely to leave me alone. So I decided to figure out which label would fit me best. Two, in particular, seemed ideal: capitalist-roader and reactionary capitalist academic authority.

To qualify as a capitalist-roader, you had to be in a position of authority. Being the head of my department would certainly count, even if it was only a modest post. Was I actually walking the road of capitalism? That was a trickier question, but since everyone in a position of authority had already been labeled a capitalist-roader, I would probably count as one too.

I was considered an authority in my field, a top-ranked professor who served in the Chinese Academy of Sciences. Twenty years of political education had taught me that individualism was at the heart of capitalism, and I readily admitted to defending my own personal interests. Capitalists were, by definition, reactionary, which made me a reactionary capitalist academic authority, irrespective of the actual quality of my academic work. Now that I had chosen my own political label, I would almost have been offended if anyone disagreed with me. As a line in a poem by the eighth-century poet Han Yu puts it: "It is indeed true that I deserve to die, O Emperor."

From the 1950s onward, all of China had studied two forms of conflict: enemy conflict and internal conflict, or conflict within the people. I, too, had spent years discussing these concepts and making enthusiastic speeches in study meetings. But not until the Cultural Revolution did I ever think about applying any of these theories to my own life. What I wondered was: Did this particular label make me an enemy of the people? Mao said that enemy conflict should be handled in an authoritarian manner, whereas internal conflict should be handled democratically by the masses through criticism, so I was anxious to figure out which approach applied in my own case.

We all agreed that the Communist Liberation had improved everyone's lives. Everyone, that is, except for the counterrevolutionary enemies of the people, who lived in constant fear of being persecuted. Even though I knew this to be the case, I didn't actually care until I seemed set to be labeled a counterrevolutionary myself, and the question of what counterrevolutionary activity was ceased to be strictly theoretical for me. The newspapers emphasized how important it was to distinguish correctly between enemy and internal conflict, but I still found the difference confusing. There seemed to be neither a qualitatively nor a quantitatively definitive approach to the question. If this was merely a philosophical distinction, what were its practical implications? And if conflict was a legal concept, why wasn't it enshrined by law? I had spent five years in the National People's Congress and had never come across any legislation that addressed the two forms of conflict. Although I had no interest in following the shifting political winds that governed these amorphous debates, I spent days pondering this question, which was not a theoretical question now that it was relevant to my own life.

I had never seriously thought about political labels and used to ignore them because they had nothing to do with me. New hats were invented with each political campaign. The victims weren't ever allowed to choose their own hats, and they always accepted the hats they were given. I never once gave a thought to the feelings of the people wearing hats. But now that I was thinking about it, I realized I could no more avoid being given a hat than I could leave the house without a hat in the winter. No one knew how the god of labels divvied them up.

I hadn't been publicly denounced, beaten up, or even formally stripped of my position as department head, nor did I have any actual authority, and certain sidelong attacks began to cause me trouble. I once found a notice in the Foreign Languages Department addressed directly to me: "Ji Xianlin, you are required to hand over three thousand yuan." Disappointingly, the notice addressed me by name without calling me a capitalist-roader or counterrevolutionary. But an order was an order, so I immediately took three thousand yuan to the student dorm room listed on the notice. I smiled politely as I handed a stack of banknotes to the students there, but they didn't smile. To my surprise, they also refused to accept the money. "Take it away!" they said. I obeyed.

One day when I was sitting at home and reading, several Red Guards barged in and declared that they were about to "destroy the Four Olds." The Four Olds? I wondered. But there was no time to find out what they meant, so all I could do was let the students have their way. It turned out that their targets were the many little ornaments that stood on my desk and bedside table, or pictures hanging on the walls. The Red Guards represented the "direction of the revolution," so if they said something was a Four Old, I obediently took it and smashed it to pieces. Within half an hour, I had destroyed many of the things I treasured most. One of them stands out in my memory: a black clay figurine of a smiling chubby baby, which I had brought home from Wuxi. The Red Guards also discovered that the portrait of the Great Leader on the wall wasn't dusty, and said that I must have put it up very recently. They were actually right. But I quickly replied that it was particularly clean because I always dusted it carefully. I was impressed by their eye for detail.

When the madness was at its peak, I figured we might as well simply destroy the planet itself, the oldest thing in existence. I heard stories of the Four Olds being destroyed all over the country. One professor told me that two paintings he owned by the artists Qi Baishi and Wang Xuetao were both destroyed.[1] But that is only the tip of the iceberg: No one knows how many priceless pieces of art were destroyed. If the Red Guards had truly succeeded in exterminating the Four Olds, what would be left of our artistic heritage? What legacy would we now be striving so hard to preserve?

I couldn't get the matter of labels out of my mind. I could tell that I was vulnerable to being labeled a reactionary capitalist academic authority, the very label I myself had thought suited me best. That would theoretically make me a capitalist enemy of the people, but the directives also said that enemy conflict could sometimes be resolved internally. That was why I hadn't been struggled against yet.

The masses didn't forget about me. They occasionally invited me to a criticism meeting.[2] These meetings were less brutal than struggle sessions, and I was usually criticized for the "revisionist" tendency of prioritizing intellectual and academic work above everything else. This was apparently revisionist the way enjoying springtime was revisionist. Under my leadership, the entire Eastern Languages Department was susceptible to that criticism—we were apparently all hardworking to a fault. I couldn't deny that fact: In every political campaign since Liberation, I had stood up in criticism meetings and criticized my own "revisionist tendency to prioritize academics," and so far I had always gotten away with it. But after making all those speeches, I always crept back into my old work habits; I know that everything I've accomplished so far is the result of revisionist hard work. So if being labeled a capitalist-roader was a tribute to my diligence, I would be happy to accept the label as an indirect compliment. For the time being I knew that I was lucky: Like a wild bird that a boy with a stone can strike down at any moment, as long as I was still in flight I was free.

# A HALF-YEAR RESPITE

HALFWAY UP MOUNT Tai, one of the five Taoist sacred mountains, there is a mile-long stretch where the steep path suddenly becomes flat, and every hiker remembers this as a welcome break from the arduous climb. During the steep climb that was the Cultural Revolution, the half year from the end of 1966 to midway through 1967 was a relatively flat stretch for me. Although Yanyuan was caught up in the fever sweeping the country, for the time being I was safe. I was grateful for the flat ground under my feet and the chance to catch my breath.

I had never previously considered philosophical questions such as the place of man in the universe or the place of the individual in society. But after Liberation, each successive political movement forced you to reconsider the security of your own position. Everyone was either a persecutor or being persecuted. And as political movements evolved, the groups were constantly splintering and regrouping, so that the persecutors could easily become the persecuted in the next stage of the struggle and vice versa. The position of each individual shifted constantly, like a dizzyingly complex military formation.

I was constantly troubled by the question of my own position and of how I myself was going to be labeled. I was relieved to eventually realize that I had not been labeled an enemy of the people. I was still one of the people, which made a big difference as to how I would be treated. If one of the people messed something up, it could be written off as a simple mistake. But if an enemy made a slip of the tongue, if he said socialism when he meant capitalism, or vice versa, then he would be labeled an active counterrevolutionary and become the target of a struggle session. It was never clear who had the authority to choose the enemies of the people or what counted as enemy conflict. I couldn't grasp the difference between enemy and internal conflict, and was constantly afraid that I would fall off the edge and find that I had become an irredeemable enemy.

I had, at some point, ceased to be the department head, though it was unclear if or when I had been dismissed. The slogan of the times was: "There is no crime in revolution, it is reasonable to revolt!" Even the former president of the republic, Liu Shaoqi, could be displaced without due process in the name of revolution, never mind a lowly department head such as myself. I counted myself lucky to have lost the title of department head without having acquired any other labels in return.

By then, the university was swarming with troops from the army's thought propaganda team, who had been sent to "support the leftists." Each department hosted several officers and troop members. The revolutionaries in each department also set up their own leadership. Teachers and students from good class backgrounds who were enthusiastic about enforcing the class struggle would tie a bit of red cloth around their arms, which marked them as revolutionaries. To have a good class background, you had to be a peasant or a worker, or come from a family of revolutionary martyrs or party functionaries. These people were the rightful leaders of the revolution. They were joined by others who had had the foresight to oppose Lu Ping during the Socialist Education Movement, but for some reason, the latter weren't allowed to wear red armbands. No one pretended to be a revolutionary by wearing a fake armband. The children of Party cadres were in a tricky situation. They certainly considered themselves the reddest of the Red Guards and insisted on wearing armbands of red silk while everyone else used plain red cloth. But their position was also more precarious. If their parents or siblings fell out of favor, they would be branded "children of blackguards" and fall out of favor instantly.

The opposition to Lu Ping had first come about in 1964, during the Socialist Education Movement, when faculty and students at Peking University were influenced by extreme leftist thinking to conclude that the university president, Lu Ping, was a revisionist. This conclusion sparked a huge revolt, and I'm afraid I was part of it. The more we found out about how the university functioned, the more passionate we became. We all felt that the institution was rotting from within. In my naïveté, I thought that opposing Lu Ping would help to preserve the direction of the revolution. I held no grudge against Lu Ping—in fact, we got along well, and he had been kind to me. But I told myself that I had to put my own feelings aside for the sake of the revolution. Lu Ping's name was later cleared at the International Hotel Conference, and no one was punished for having opposed him. Nonetheless, I reflected on my involvement in the matter and decided to make a public self-criticism. Shortly thereafter, in the autumn of 1965, I was sent to Nankou Village.

Then the thought propaganda team moved in, and the cadres in the Eastern Languages Department were reorganized. I had escaped the first wave of persecution in the Cultural Revolution, and as one of those who had opposed Lu Ping, I should have been named a "revolutionary cadre." Instead it was said that I had given in to Lu Ping, that my stance toward class struggle had faltered, and that I had to be excluded. The cadres who had not self-criticized following the International Hotel Conference were now treated as heroes, with seats on the revolutionary committees of their departments and even that of the university. I didn't care for these honors, but I feared for my safety. A Red Guard who knew me well told me that he had seen the army's internal documents and that in them I was classified as an individual "on the edge"—somewhere between an enemy and a merely errant member of the people. I felt relieved to be on the right side at the moment but disturbed by my perilous position.

Since traveling by rail was now free, people started making revolution everywhere, going on all kinds of long trips in the name of revolution. The stations were packed with people, and anyone who was bold enough to hoist themselves out of the crowd through the window of a train compartment could go wherever they wanted. We were told that all this was "lighting the fire of revolution." Eventually, the whole country was in chaos. Someone said this was a deliberate tactic to confuse our enemies, but we didn't confuse anyone but ourselves. At the time I was still a wholehearted supporter of the revolution.

As the source and center of the Cultural Revolution, Peking University attracted scores of these revolutionary pilgrims. We treated them as important guests and did our best to welcome them. Most departments had been assigned responsibility for one of the blocks in which our guests were housed. To demonstrate my loyalty and gratitude for not having been classified as an enemy, I volunteered to take the night shift at the visitors' camp. The guests had no blankets, so my colleagues and I brought them blankets from our own homes. I noticed that they had no basins, so I bought twenty with my own money, and took pleasure in handing them out. But the revolutionaries, both the young and the young at heart among them, turned out to be inconsiderate guests who ripped our blankets and chipped the new basins. Although I had been genuinely enthusiastic about welcoming them, my zeal faded.

Eventually, the authorities realized that the whole thing had gone too far; some villages had ceased agricultural production altogether. They decreed that the tourists had to be sent back to their homes, to "make revolution by increasing production." The thought propaganda teams at Peking University were responsible for conveying this message to our guests. As part of this initiative, our department would visit places where large numbers of guests lodged and persuade them to go home, beginning at the Xiyi Hotel near campus. But having been treated so well, why would these traveling revolutionaries leave of their own accord? At the hotel we pleaded, argued, and sometimes even quarreled with the guests. I talked myself hoarse and still had to remain extremely polite. Gradually the guests began to make their way home.

Next we went to the Bureau of Meteorology and had the same arguments with the guests there. I had seen thousands of big-character posters and was bored by most of them. But I was struck by the big-character posters at the bureau. Many of them said the usual things, but a few were truly startling: "Cut So-and-so into a thousand pieces!" "Boil So-and-so alive in a vat of oil!" Perhaps their unusually vivid imagery was borrowed from the Buddhist hell. I also had the good fortune to witness an unforgettable struggle session. A little car drove up, and a capitalist-roader in a well-ironed suit—a bureau chief, perhaps—got out. He took a curious little paper hat from the backseat of the car and put it carefully on his head. The hat was hung with all kinds of trinkets, including a tortoise that wobbled whenever he took a step. As soon as he entered the hall a roar of slogans arose, followed by endless speeches criticizing the man. When the whole process had been completed, the capitalist-roader left the hall, got back into the car, and took his hat off, carefully placing it on the backseat for future use. I found this man more enigmatic than the Mona Lisa. He never stopped smiling even after being rhetorically cut into a thousand pieces and boiled in oil.

In the winter we were sent farther afield to communicate the official message to yet more visitors. I had to commute an hour by bike to the place where we worked, and it took two hours to walk there when it snowed. We didn't have so much as a room to ourselves, so we ate under a canopy we built in the yard. The lukewarm rice would freeze as soon as it touched our bowls. Su Wu, the Han dynasty diplomat exiled to Siberia, must have eaten rice like this, with ice crushed into it. Despite the hardship, I was still in good spirits, secretly relieved not to have been categorized as a capitalist-roader.

When we had successfully completed our mission and the visitors had all left, we returned to campus. Another memorable event was taking place: the Haidian district elections. These elections were for the local assemblies, which would elect representatives to the provincial-level assemblies, which in turn would elect deputies to the National People's Congress. So this lowest level of representatives, while relatively insignificant, was also the most democratically elected, and hence the most heavily contested. I had sat on the People's Political Consultative Conference and served as a Beijing deputy to the National People's Congress. I had even run in the Haidian district elections a couple of times. I had never considered the privilege of voting in the elections to be an achievement in itself. But after the first round of capitalist-roaders had been purged, many people lost their voting rights. So when I saw my name sparkling on the list of eligible voters, I was as happy as a scholar in imperial times finding his name on a list of successful examination candidates. Retaining this privilege had been no mean feat. I celebrated the election day by wearing new clothes to the polling station, and savored the weight of the red ballot in my hand. I felt incredibly lucky not to have become an untouchable.

Later on we were sent to a village south of Beijing, near Nanyuan, to help with the harvest, which was also led by revolutionary cadres and the thought propaganda team. 1966 was a wet year. We spent two weeks in the village, and it rained nearly every day. All day long we would carry sheaves of wheat from the fields back to the village to be dried in the sun before threshing. When it rained we would hurry to cover the wheat with canvas until the rain passed and we could pull the canvas off to let the wheat dry. We sometimes did this several times a day, and if it rained at night, we would get up and race outside to drape canvas over the crops. We were constantly drenched in sweat and rain while all the farmers sat in the people's commune enjoying free meals; not one of them came to join us in the fields. Those of us who had come prepared to "learn from the peasants," as the slogan went, began to wonder what we could learn from them. I used to devour novels about peasant life, but when I realized that the depiction of the peasants' political consciousness was completely exaggerated, I began to find these novels contrived and stopped reading them.

As an imposter among the masses, I worked especially hard. I carried as many sheaves of wheat back to the village as the youngest and fittest men on the team, and was proud when the department commended me for my efforts. Our living conditions were very basic. After a long day of hard work, we all slept on mats in a large warehouse at night. Many people had brought mosquito nets and repellent, but I had none, so I often woke in the morning covered with mosquito bites. I felt like the child in the traditional story about filial piety who deliberately exposed himself to the mosquitoes so that his parents wouldn't be bitten.

We enjoyed our time in the fields. One day, someone spotted a wild rabbit, and we all took part in the chase, until one of us broke the rabbit's leg and we managed to catch it. Those of us who had a weakness for snake meat would catch a snake a day, run back to the village, and grill it on the spot. The half-year respite passed happily, but it wouldn't last forever.

# JOINING THE FRAY

BY THE AUTUMN of 1967, the Red Guards and other revolutionaries had long since separated into factions. The *Romance of the Three Kingdoms* was right: The long-divided will inevitably be united, and the long-united will become divided. It was time for divisions again.

Not long before, the revolutionaries at Peking University had been united in a single revolutionary organization, the New Peking University Commune, called the New Beida for short. It was headed by the Empress Dowager, Nie Yuanzi, who was said to be a "Type 38 rifle," belonging to the generation of cadres who had joined the Party at the beginning of the Second World War. Despite being middle-aged, she always dressed provocatively. Her performance at Peking University had been mediocre. Originally the deputy head of the Economics Department, she was then transferred to the Philosophy Department as its Party branch secretary. She had enough political savvy to have written the first Marxist-Leninist poster at just the right moment, and the support of Party leaders catapulted her into the national spotlight. I knew her to be arrogant, dim-witted, stubborn, and crafty. Every time she opened her mouth, her supporters worried that she would make a fool of herself. This was the woman who had free rein to do anything she liked in Yanyuan.

As the Great Leader said, "Oppression always begets resistance." Students who found Nie Yuanzi's regime oppressive began to start their own revolutionary groups. They mostly called themselves the Such-and-such squadrons, with names taken from Mao Zedong's poems. There was the Fight the Nationalists Squadron, the Pluck the Moon from the Skies Squadron, the Mountain Scalers.... Soon all the best lines had been taken, and new groups found themselves at a loss for poetic revolutionary names. The squadrons ranged in size from four or five to dozens of students. It was said that there was even a squadron of one. To start one, all you had to do was put up a poster that read, "The east wind blows, the drums resound, only the winner will be left standing!" and yell a few slogans. Soon there were so many groups that even the renowned essayist and historian Hu Shi would have despaired of counting them.[1]

There were also more and more big-character posters, and since the walls and temporary stands had long been pasted over, new bamboo stands were constantly being built. Apart from announcing new squadrons, the posters also criticized various capitalist counterrevolutionaries. Some of them were only four or five pages long; others stretched to nine, ten, or a hundred pages, and kept growing longer. Nearby residents made a living selling old posters for scrap paper. Some students practiced their calligraphy by designing posters, and I noticed that the handwriting was improving over time—furthering the practice of this traditional art form was surely an unintended side effect of the Cultural Revolution.

Individual squadrons began to form alliances and join forces, eventually amalgamating into two big camps: New Beida, the original group, and Jinggangshan, the upstart, named after the birthplace of the Red Army in the mountains of Jiangxi Province. The former was in government, so to speak, and the latter in opposition; they argued constantly through their respective posters. But unlike in a political system such as the British one, there was no pretense of fair play. Rather, it was the norm to spread malicious rumors about your opponents. Partisan politics ruined friendships and tore families apart. We fought each other more ferociously than we had ever fought our capitalist enemies. One poster read: "I would die to protect Nie Yuanzi and Sun Fengyi!" If only we had invested all this energy into industrialization and the modernization of agriculture, China would long since have become Asia's leading economic power.

At the time, we were all blinded by partisanship, and it was impossible to judge the two factions objectively. But now that so much time has passed, I think it can fairly be said that the two factions were more or less the same. Both were composed mostly of younger lecturers and students. Both supposedly had a political platform, though the actual content thereof was rather opaque. Both subscribed to extreme leftist thinking. Both fought constantly, raided houses, and wreaked destruction. If a lecturer or cadre was struggled by both factions, the two struggle sessions looked exactly the same. Both groups were ruthless and equally sadistic. They beat their victims using bicycle chains wrapped in rubber, which drew no blood, so that no one could accuse them of having done wrong. Both revered Madame Mao, Jiang Qing, and claimed to be her most loyal followers. New Beida attempted to intimidate its opponents by invoking her name, and Jinggangshan also flew the flag of devotion to Jiang Qing. There was only one clear difference between them: New Beida was in power, and Jinggangshan was the underdog, which is a position more likely to provoke sympathy.

As far as I could tell, since their political platforms were identical, their struggle could only have been about power rather than policy. Both were desperate to gain power and destroy the opposing faction along the way. Both did their best to recruit popular lecturers and cadres. Jinggangshan controlled a handful of student dorms, and New Beida controlled the rest of the campus. The dorms were heavily guarded. The better-funded New Beida sawed off precious sections of steel pipe and sharpened them into makeshift spears that were more than sufficient for launching an attack on Jinggangshan. The latter responded by fashioning its own weapons. Both factions were said to have explosives experts among them. Their rudimentary weapons allowed them to get into armed skirmishes, including one in which a secondary-school student was killed by spear-wielding New Beida supporters.

But the Red Guards were young students, almost children, and they could never resist a good joke. Once, during an intensely heated debate in the cafeteria, when both crowds were shouting at the top of their lungs, several pairs of old shoes strung together suddenly dropped from a large crossbeam. As everyone in the university knew, "old shoes" is northern slang for a prostitute, and the phrase happened to be one of Nie Yuanzi's many nicknames. Although the crowds were ready to tear each other to pieces, the unexpected interlude made them burst into laughter, and the debate fizzled out. Soon the windows of Jinggangshan dorms were festooned with worn-out shoes.

At another debate in the cafeteria, the leaders of both factions were sitting on the podium, with an audience gathered in front of them. The leaders of Jinggangshan, and possibly of New Beida, were known as "orderlies." The word did have a democratic, revolutionary ring to it, as when all societal titles were democratized after the French Revolution. There was an elderly professor onstage, a respected specialist in fluid dynamics and the theory of relativity. He was a man of integrity whom the students respected, and one of the few people whom Party leaders were keen to protect. I was told that when New Beida heard this man disapproved of what the Empress Dowager was doing, they not only sent people to his home to harass him but threatened and blackmailed him over the phone. He originally had no intention of joining Jinggangshan but was so put off by New Beida's threats that he changed his mind. He was immediately named an

orderly, and at this debate he was the oldest person onstage. There
were many subjects of debate, and the cafeteria was crowded with
students from both factions, each side utterly certain that it was in
the right and its opponents in the wrong. The sight reminded me of
televised U.S. presidential debates, with hordes of supporters clap-
ping and cheering. The atmosphere was tense and very lively.

Yanyuan had descended into a state of chaos officially said to
"confuse the enemy," but we hardly knew who our enemies were.
Eventually, two bigger factions formed across China, in Beijing the
Sky Faction and elsewhere the Earth Faction. Both insisted that they
were the only true revolutionaries, and troops sent to support the
leftists couldn't decide who the leftists were. Soon even the army itself split into factions in some places. We declared that chaos confuses the enemy, but we were confusing no one but ourselves; if any
enemies were watching, they would have sat back and smiled.

I myself would have to stay out of the fray and remain neutral if I
wanted to preserve my freedom. That way I could also avoid having
to worry about getting involved in politics and making passionate
speeches. Since classes had been canceled, I didn't need to teach nor
do any research. I could stroll around reading posters and listening
to debates.

But utopias don't exist, and Yanyuan certainly wasn't one. I
couldn't ignore what was happening around me; I had to react. As
the saying goes, a tall tree is swayed by the wind. For the past twenty
years, I had served as the head of my department and held other political offices, such as that of Beijing deputy to the National People's
Congress, and although I wasn't the tallest tree around, I could feel
the effect of the political winds. I also had a keenly developed sense
of justice, and I was very stubborn. Even with a safe haven in sight, I
would rather sail out into a storm.

I began to realize that I disagreed with Nie Yuanzi. I felt that her
actions were contrary to the direction of the revolution. I may not

have known where the revolution was heading, but I had spent more than a decade studying Marxism-Leninism and knew that "serving the people" was a crucial measure of good Communist leadership. It could not be said of the Empress Dowager that she served the people. She enjoyed her privileges too much, loved giving orders, and often made life difficult for people who disagreed with her by firing them or withholding their pay. She called for people to be struggled against, allowing them to be tortured and killed. She had already been responsible for a few deaths, such as that of the secondary-school student I have mentioned above. New Beida, the organization she headed, was the most powerful organization on campus. Later, when revolutionary committees were established according to Party guidelines, she gained power officially as the chairperson of Peking University's revolutionary committee. All these honors only made her more arrogant; the more I watched her have her way, the less able I was to hold my peace. But I also knew that it would be dangerous to make an enemy of her, so I remained neutral.

At this time, a mob burned down the Chinese embassy in Jakarta, sparking large-scale protests at the Indonesian embassy in Beijing. Both factions seized this opportunity to show off and rented several dozen cars that idled along the road leading to the south gate of campus, waiting to take protesters to the embassy. Since I didn't belong to either faction, I didn't have a ride, and both factions invited me to ride with them. I would have accepted an invitation from a woman in Jinggangshan, but I still had reservations about aligning myself with the opposition and didn't want to act rashly. Instead I got into a New Beida car. The roads were packed with people waving red flags. We got to the embassy, chanted slogans for a while, and went back to campus.

I also followed the crowds to the home of a high-ranking army general to make revolution. I wasn't sure why he was being targeted, but I tagged along anyway. It wasn't that the Red Guards ever needed a good reason, but they usually did have the implicit approval of someone powerful. His house was near campus, by Jade Spring Hill, so most people walked there, and I rode my bike, "going it alone"[2] in a horde of cyclists that could have belonged to either faction, glad not to have to choose between the two factions again. At Green Dragon Bridge, I saw people headed toward West Mountain and decided to follow them. It wasn't until we reached Wan An Cemetery, behind Jade Spring Hill, that I realized we must have overshot the turn. By the time we got back to the bridge, someone in the crowd was shouting that we had already successfully made revolution, so I followed the crowds back to Yanyuan without so much as having seen the doors of the general's house. This, I realized, must be what most people's experience of making revolution was like.

Both factions organized political classes for cadres as a means of competing for their allegiance. Even cadres who had previously been labeled capitalist-roaders or removed from their posts were being targeted, and I was among them. Again I hesitated to join a Jinggangshan class since New Beida was in power. They had many more members and a vindictive leader, and I knew what would happen if I offended them by being seen at Jinggangshan. The classes were identical: both extolled the Great Leader and professed a startling degree of devotion toward Madame Mao, who was praised in big-character posters and adored like the Virgin Mary. Although I had heard some criticism of her by then, I was naïve enough to continue supporting her.

But since I wasn't good at keeping my opinions to myself, people gradually got to know what I thought of the two factions, which caused problems for me. Students from each group took turns recruiting me to their side, playing good cop/bad cop. The New Beida students came to my home and office (now that I think about it, it seems strange that I should still have had an office, but I distinctly recall seeing them there). The polite ones merely warned me not to join Jinggangshan, while the less polite said things like "Don't join them if you value your life!" They phoned me at home to cajole me into joining them. I realized that I was in the same situation as the elderly professor I mentioned earlier. I was troubled by the New Beida's supporters, and the more cornered I felt, the less I felt like having anything to do with them. Eventually I decided to take the plunge and join Jinggangshan, even though I was well aware of how dangerous it was. I wrote in my diary: "I would die to protect the direction of the Great Leader's revolution!"

The Jinggangshan students were delighted. Unusually, they decided to appoint me an orderly of their Ninth Brigade (comprising members of my department). I was glad I had decided to join them, but one unfortunate consequence of the decision was that I too became caught up in partisan fever since I no longer had to hide my opinions. Along with other Jinggangshan students, I started writing big-character posters and making speeches attacking New Beida. I must admit that we weren't always well mannered and not everything we said was true.

I still cherished hopes that I might be one of the lucky few who would escape. I reasoned that although I used to be apolitical and knew little about the Communist Party, I had never been in the Kuomintang or any other counterrevolutionary organization. There would be nothing for my enemies to attack because I had nothing to hide.

But I also knew that Nie Yuanzi was especially hostile toward me. She had always been a vengeful person, and she was now at the height of her political career as an alternate member of the Central Party Committee and deputy chair of the Beijing Revolutionary Committee. She never put up with any opposition. At the time, getting one word wrong would suffice to brand you a counterrevolutionary—for instance, if you happened to have stored the words "socialist" and "capitalist" in the same mental card file, using one when you meant the other could prove a fatal error. Your opponents would immediately seize on the slip of your tongue and fabricate arbitrary meta-physical misreadings of your words. And yet the Empress Dowager herself often made such mistakes.

I was aware that I was walking a fine line. Throughout the summer and autumn months of 1967, it was rumored that I was next, that my home would be raided. I wanted to ignore the rumors but couldn't help overhearing them. Every week I wrote in my diary: "There's a storm brewing above my head." Eventually, I knew, the storm was going to crush me. All the lecturers who dared to oppose New Beida were feeling this way. Throughout that sultry summer and dreary autumn, I felt uneasy.

# A HOUSE RAID

DESPITE THE RUMORS, I kept hoping that my luck would hold. I told myself that I had no "pigtails" or weaknesses that could easily be attacked. I was wrong.

On the night of November 30, 1967, I had taken a sleeping pill and was fast asleep when a car pulled up outside. I heard an impatient rapping at the door and opened it to find six men holding wooden cudgels. They were all Nie Yuanzi's disciples and students in my department, their faces arrogant and frosty. I had long expected this, so I wasn't surprised. As the proverb goes, "The hero knows when not to resist." I am no hero, but I refused to give these men a reason to use their cudgels by resisting their entrance. Chairman Mao had proclaimed: "There is no crime in revolution, it is reasonable to revolt!" People chanted this slogan every day without thinking about what "revolution" or "revolt" actually meant. All kinds of crimes could be committed in broad daylight in the name of revolution. Although I had tried my best to protect the direction of the Great Leader's revolution, the revolution itself had now decided I would be struggled against next. Even then, however, I was too loyal to question it.

I was hustled into the kitchen before I could get dressed. My wife and elderly aunt were being held there already. We shivered in the piercing draft. I couldn't tell what they were thinking because the men were waving cudgels in our faces, and we weren't allowed to speak. My mind was clear. I knew that any gesture of kindness had long been branded "revisionist." Chinese philosophy had debated whether human nature is intrinsically good or evil for millennia, and until then, I would have sided with the notion of innate goodness. But when my house was raided, I changed my mind. Could you believe that these people were innately good? Could you deny that they were acting like beasts? Anyone with a conscience should be concerned by the ethical decline of Chinese society today, and yet we seldom ask how it began.

Of course, some of these thoughts only occurred to me later. At the time I was determined neither to grovel to the Red Guards nor to resist them. There is no use reasoning with beasts. So I crouched on the dusty kitchen floor, watching and listening. I wondered why they had sent such a large team to the home of three unarmed elderly people. Of the two men guarding the kitchen, one was a student of mine called Gu. He had been a student of Korean language and history in my department, but now we were enemies. Red Guards were never prosecuted for any deaths they caused, and their cudgels and spears were the law.

Chinese robbers traditionally blindfolded their victims and poured cooking oil in their ears. Fortunately we had not covered these customs in class, so even though I couldn't see what was happening outside, I could hear it. The Red Guards were making such a clatter that the tiles trembled on the roof. If I had the Buddhist power of seeing through walls, I would find our visitors peering under mattresses, opening boxes, and ransacking cupboards. They smashed and destroyed as they saw fit, and they didn't need keys when they could hack both wood and metal open with their axes. I had lived frugally for years and saved enough to buy a few antiques on occasion. They were destroyed right away. These hooligans were experts at house raiding, and the Cultural Revolution had given them ample opportunity to hone their skills.

One man named Wang, who was studying Thai, asked me for the keys to the bike storage. Having been to my home before, he knew that all my books were kept downstairs. The administrators of the staff quarters had been worried that they would be too heavy for the floors in my apartment and persuaded me to move them to the bike storage on the ground floor. The bike storage space would have sufficed for our building if we had only a few bikes among us, but since there were far too many bikes to fit in such a small space, it had fallen into disuse and lay empty. I had my neighbors' permission to move my books there instead. The Red Guards had already made a thorough search of the apartment, and when Wang stretched out his hand for the key to the bike storage, I could tell he was an expert. Again, I felt as though I could see and hear through walls, as though I were watching the destruction of my beloved library.

The Red Guards may not have been exceptional students, but they would have been familiar with the imperial practice of "obliterating the nine branches of the family," slaughtering anyone who had a connection with the accused. In any case, they made me hand over the little address book in which I had recorded all my friends' names. I feared for my innocent friends and relatives who were unlucky enough to be in my book. My heart was bleeding.

I cowered in the kitchen, my thoughts churning. I was distressed and outraged, terrified and then instantly calm. Our lives lay entirely in the hands of these men. We were like ants beneath their fingertips, and heaven could not hear our cries. The world seemed to be ruled not by men but by ghouls or beasts. I thought of Shakuntala in the classical Indian play, whose goddess mother swoops down from the heavens to rescue her when she has nowhere to go. In a world without gods, who would rescue me?

Time is indifferent to human joys and sadnesses. The night passed, the house grew quiet, and our guards disappeared. The car roared away, and soon the night was as still as though nothing had ever happened. We were left to survey the battlefield.

The rooms were a mess. All the tables and chairs had been overturned. Anything that could be broken was broken, including all the antiques and other decorations. My bed had been thoroughly searched, and someone had stepped on the sturdy hot water bottle under the covers, thoroughly soaking the bed. Despite having been up all night, we were wide awake, but numb, speechless, paralyzed.

A popular saying came to mind: A misunderstanding is when a good man strikes a good man; an ordeal is when a bad man strikes a good man; a comeuppance is when a good man strikes a bad man; and a squabble is when a bad man strikes a bad man. Despite my many shortcomings, I believe I am a good man. I am considerate, I care about those around me, and unlike the legendary general Cao Cao, I would never claim that I would "rather wrong all men than have all men wrong me." I think I fit the general definition of a good person. There may have been some good people led astray among the hooligans who raided my home. But many of the others were psychopaths indulging their sadistic instincts under the cover of revolutionary instructions. I had previously worshipped the notion of making revolution, but now I see it as nothing but the most ignorant, the most unprincipled form of metaphysical sophistry. Unfortunately hundreds of thousands of young people were infected by this fever, and many have now reached middle age. The Red Guards have done well for themselves: some have made millions, others have married into wealth, and yet others have successfully scaled the slippery slope of the Party bureaucracy. And yet, strangely, none of them appear to regret their deeds! Are they all profoundly forgetful or have they no conscience?

It had been the longest night of my life, but dawn finally came. At daybreak I got on my bike and pedaled to Jinggangshan headquarters, naïvely hoping that my own faction would take up my cause. All the loudspeakers in Peking University were blaring my name and broadcasting my crimes. I can't be worth their going to all this trouble, I thought. It made me feel tiny, riding my bike alone through campus while the loudspeakers cried, "Down with Ji Xianlin!" Even today, that scene strikes me as being both ridiculous and pitiable. I was now a legitimate target.

When I got to the headquarters, I found that Jinggangshan's leaders already knew of the raid. In fact, they were sending a photographer to my home to record the carnage. I would later learn that they were already preparing to investigate my record so that they could toss me overboard and denounce me when the time came. While I was loyal to them, they were doing their best to get rid of me. When I left the building, I found that my bicycle had been locked to a tree trunk, probably by someone from New Beida. I had to say farewell to the bike that had accompanied me everywhere for more than twenty years, and return home on foot.

There I found the Jinggangshan photographer looking through my garbage. I knew that he had political rather than aesthetic motivations. He wanted to see whether New Beida had made any errors in the course of the raid. Had they stepped on a piece of newspaper with the Great Leader's photograph on it? Had they torn or stained any images of the Great Leader? These were all severe offenses, and if he found any evidence of them, the photographs could be used against New Beida in the future. But the Red Guards were expert house-raiders, and the disappointed photographer had to leave empty-handed.

The Jinggangshan leaders appeared to be sympathetic to me after the raid, and I began to think that I should stay at the headquarters for safety. Later I realized that would have put me in even greater danger. But at the time, I was afraid that New Beida would send someone to arrest me at night and hold me in a secret location, which had happened to other victims. Jinggangshan was at least heavily guarded. But then again, although I didn't know yet that my own faction was planning to investigate me, I knew that they had investigated N., the elderly professor from my department, whose background was considered complicated because he had lived overseas. I reasoned that there was nothing to stop them from investigating me. Now that New Beida had struck me down, I was dead weight, which meant they would do anything to get rid of me. It was true I had done nothing wrong, but I knew that factionalism can drive people to do treacherous things. Instead of facing the potentially embarrassing scenario of being kicked out by my own faction, I decided to go home and wait for the ax to fall. The catastrophe I had feared all year had finally hit. There seemed to be no place anywhere in the whole wide world for me. Upon his execution, the seventeenth-century writer Jin Shengtan is said to have exclaimed, "Being beheaded is the most painful thing that can possibly happen to someone, and here I have achieved it with little effort—isn't that something?" I, too, had achieved my infamy with scant effort, but I could hardly bring myself to take pleasure in that fact.

Overnight I had ceased to be one of the masses and had been branded a counterrevolutionary element. New Beida leaders in my department told me to wait at home and be ready to report at any time. I waited at home for days, but nothing happened. Years later I was told that New Beida had wanted to arrest me but lacked the necessary evidence, so they had raided my rooms preemptively in hopes of finding what they needed among my confiscated possessions. The strategy worked. A few days later, their Red Guards came triumphantly to my rooms and took me away to be interrogated at the Foreign Languages Building. All my decades working in that very building and serving as department head had come to this.

I was permitted to sit down during that first interrogation. I was furious and refused to cooperate, reasoning that I had done nothing wrong. As the proverb says, "Catching a tiger is easy, setting it free is difficult," and I figured that my captors would eventually realize they had to set me free. I even raised my voice, and my interrogators—some of whom were my own students—looked embarrassed. But their tone eventually grew harsher, perhaps because they had discovered more "proof" of my crimes. I have often wanted to ask my interrogators: Surely you couldn't have believed all the accusations you made against me?

The first piece of evidence they presented was a basket with half-burned letters, which was said to prove that I had attempted to destroy top secret documents. The truth was that after the Cultural Revolution began, I realized that I would be hard-pressed to justify occupying four rooms in the building where we lived, so I gave one of the two larger rooms to a friend of mine who lived downstairs and another to a woman in New Beida from a good class background. With less storage space, I decided to burn some of my old letters. I did so openly, but a Red Guard stopped me and convinced me to put the remaining letters in a bamboo basket. I explained this to my interrogators but was only told to stop being uncooperative. The second piece of evidence was a kitchen knife they had found under my aunt's pillow. Since the revolution began, the crime rate had spiked, and it was said that burglars would go straight to the kitchen and find a kitchen knife they could use to threaten their victims. My elderly aunt was terrified of burglars, so she always kept the kitchen knife under her pillow at night. My interrogators said that the knife had been found under my pillow and that I was planning to murder the Red Guards. Again, I told them the truth, but they simply said I was being uncooperative. The third piece of evidence was a photograph of Chiang Kai-shek and Soong Mei-ling, given to me by a Chinese student called Zhang when we were both studying in Göttingen. He may have been a member of the Kuomintang's Three People's Principles Youth Corps or Blue Shirts Society. I had opposed Chiang ever since the student demonstrations of 1932 in Nanjing. I had no illusions that he would successfully retake the mainland: History suggests that a corrupt ruler can never regain power once he has been ousted. But unlike Comrade Chen, the policeman who burned all his correspondence, as I mentioned earlier, I kept every single bit of paper I had ever been given. Sure enough, this photograph got me in trouble. The interrogators said that I had kept it so that if the Kuomintang ever did retake mainland China, I would be able to use it to prove my loyalty to them. They hadn't gone so far as to call me a Kuomintang spy, but if I tried to explain, they would only point out that I was being uncooperative. There was nothing I could say in my defense.

# ON THE BRINK OF SUICIDE

I WAS GETTING nervous. I had assumed I was politically clean, but the Red Guards had proven to be experts at uncovering the so-called evidence of my supposed errors. I had not lost confidence in myself, but I also knew that my opponents were blinded by factionalism, and I would not be able to convince them of my innocence.

In other words, there was no way out.

I lay sleepless for nights. All day long I waited apprehensively to be interrogated, and at night, I lay awake waiting for morning. I had no appetite. The future seemed dark to me, and I had no confidence that the darkness would pass. Days went by as if in a dream. At night, I would dream of someone charging at me with my own kitchen knife and awake with a start. Dreaming that the basket of half-burned letters was ablaze and rushing toward me, I broke out in a cold sweat. I dreamed of the photo of Chiang and Soong Mei-ling. Chiang's mouth was open, dripping blood, and he bared his teeth at me, while Soong had turned into a snake woman. I nearly jumped out of bed.

Not only was I miserable; I was crippled by anxiety about the future. I could see that I was trapped and that I would pay for my opposition to the Empress Dowager. Most of my opponents were good people at heart, but I knew that partisanship would drive them to persecute me. I had served as the department chair for more than twenty years and either directly or indirectly hired all the lecturers and teachers in the department. I always strove to be fair and treat people well. I couldn't understand how a factional divide could turn us instantly into enemies. Even my own faction had turned against me. Once New Beida had struck me down, Jinggangshan sent its own Red Guards to haul me off to its secret locations to be interrogated. I had thought we were on the same side, but now that it was too late, I knew better.

I was especially wounded by the betrayal of the two students I had mentored. One of them was from a peasant family and the son of a revolutionary martyr—he was as proletariat as it gets. Although his work was mediocre, I offered him a position as my teaching assistant out of a sense of "class awareness." There was another student from an impeccable class background who never fully grasped Sanskrit. Again, so as not to allow a single "proletariat brother" to fall behind, I always paid special attention to him, calling on him more frequently in class. But now that I was an object of class struggle, these two men, both members of Jinggangshan, interrogated me, insulted me, and even pulled and twisted my ears. I knew I had brought this on myself, but I was still shocked. Even though I don't subscribe to the Confucian precept that "a teacher and student will always remain father and son," I couldn't help thinking that kindness deserves a little respect in turn.

I could see no way out of my emotional distress and political quagmire. For more than a year, I had watched as capitalist-roaders were struggled against, beaten up, insulted, and literally kicked off the podium. The victim often ended up lying on the floor, unable to move. Confucius had said that "the scholar can be killed, but he cannot be humiliated," and yet intellectuals were being humiliated to a degree unprecedented in Chinese civilization. Now that I was no longer an observer but a target of class struggle, I was about to be subjected to the same humiliation. In fact, no one else had baskets full of

47

half-burned letters, telltale kitchen knives, or photos of Chiang Kai-shek. I could neither defend myself nor stoop to a false confession. I knew that a worse fate awaited me than that of the capitalist-roaders I saw onstage.

There were only two choices open to me. I could either bear my fate or escape it. The former I didn't think I could do, and yet I could barely imagine the latter: Even crickets have a survival instinct, never mind human beings. No one would choose to kill himself if there was even the slightest chance of another way out; as things were, I resolved to use the little strength I had left to take my own life. People would call me cowardly for "alienating myself from the people" by committing suicide, but I reflected that there was no point in caring what people said about you after you were dead.

Once I had decided to commit suicide, I became clearheaded and calm. I carefully considered how to go about implementing this plan.

Scores of professors and cadres had committed suicide in the months since the Cultural Revolution had begun. One of the first was Professor Wang in the History Department. At the beginning of the revolution, the Red Guards had barged into his home and questioned him. Maybe they also beat him up, though this seems unlikely to me, because the guards were gentler and not quite as revolutionary back then. But Professor Wang was too thin-skinned to withstand even this moderate assault, too staunch a believer in the principle that "the scholar cannot be humiliated." He overdosed on sleeping pills and was immediately criticized for having committed suicide. "Down with the counterrevolutionary Wang!" screamed a controversial poster pasted on the eastern wall of the main cafeteria after his death. I knew Professor Wang to be a good man and excellent scholar, one who had risked his life joining the underground Communist movement before Liberation. I could not understand how he could possibly be a counterrevolutionary. I had sympathy for his predicament.

Then there was Cheng, the Party branch secretary of the Chinese

Department. I knew him well too. He had been a student leader in the underground Communist movement in his time, and later became a leader of the Peking University student union. Despite his youth, he was already a long-serving Party member. Yet he too killed himself. He had probably been denounced as a capitalist-roader since he was not senior enough to qualify as an academic authority. He had also been struggled against as a counterrevolutionary "devil" on June 18th and made to wear a wooden placard while laboring on campus. That was too much for him. He was said to have taken a bottle of distilled alcohol and a bottle of pesticide to the woods in the Western Hills just outside Beijing where he must have numbed himself with the alcohol before drinking the pesticide. I shuddered at the thought of him rolling on the ground in pain, the pesticide burning his stomach.

I knew of people who leaped off tall buildings and smashed themselves to pieces, or people whose bodies were ripped apart on train tracks. Although I had never seen anyone commit suicide, I had heard of countless instances and could barely imagine the inward struggle that each of these individuals must have experienced.

There were two professors who had thrown themselves into the Unnamed Lake on campus in the 1950s. The lake is so shallow that I couldn't work out how they had managed to drown themselves. Did they simply wade in waist-deep and hold their heads underwater? Professor Fang of the Philosophy Department had cut his wrists with a razor blade. The bleeding could not be stanched, and bystanders watched helplessly as he died a slow and painful death.

I thought back to ancient times and the suicide of Qu Yuan, the poet and court adviser who threw himself into the Miluo River in 278 BC. Less than a century later, the warlord Xiang Yu slit his throat when his army was surrounded on the banks of the Wu River. The idea of cutting off my own head terrified me. Surely I'd have to be very strong. It seemed far more primitive than shooting myself, which I'm sure Xiang Yu would have preferred had he had access to a handgun back then. The Germans would later apply their world-class chemical engineering to the problem of suicide; it was said that Nazi leaders all carried cyanide capsules so they could end their lives at any moment by biting into one. The Japanese, of course, are famous for hara-kiri, but since no one dies immediately of cutting their belly open, the warrior needs a second, the *kaishakunin*, who is responsible for swiping his head off. That was not an option for me. Japanese lovers have apparently been known to leap together into the mouth of a volcano. Of course this will only work if you have a local volcano.

I couldn't stop thinking about suicide. Sometimes I imagined these people so vividly that I thought I could see their corpses in front of me—a terrifying and yet alluring sight. Dying wouldn't make me happy, but there seemed to be no way to go on living.

Having never considered suicide before, I realized that if I were really going to kill myself I would need to do some serious research into suicidology. Every new branch of study requires a theoretical foundation, so I produced the following observations for my comparative study of suicide methodology:

There was no need to collect every known case of suicide. I could draw my preliminary conclusions from the few examples listed above. A historical materialist reading these cases observes that hanging oneself and jumping into a well may be the oldest methods of committing suicide, and both are still popular; as primitive societies progressed toward feudalism and capitalism, these early methods didn't die out. Cyanide is available only to fascists in industrialized countries. Hara-kiri and leaping into a volcano are unique to ancient and modern Japan and difficult to put into practice. Cutting your wrists only seems to work if you are an educated person with a basic grasp of biology—most people don't succeed. Overdosing on sleeping pills, the classic capitalist method of suicide, is in fact employed by both capitalists and socialists, or perhaps only by nervous insomniac intellectuals; peasants who spend their days in the fields don't need sleeping pills. Since Chinese medicines for insomnia are too mild to have anything beyond a soporific effect, only Western sleeping pills can be repurposed for suicide, which is why this is a "capitalist" method. Trust the capitalists to invent a safe, painless, convenient form of suicide.

So much for theory. Now for the practical application: As you may have guessed, I had settled on the capitalist method of killing myself. Given that I had already been branded a counterrevolutionary, I had no reason to avoid being further associated with capitalism. Having chosen a method, I had to decide when and where to put my plan into practice. When was easy: As soon as possible. But as for where, I had two options—at home or elsewhere. Of course, committing suicide at home would be more convenient. But my family only had two rooms, a bigger and a smaller one. I was afraid that if I lay in bed and swallowed the sleeping pills at night, my aunt and wife would be terrified when they discovered my lifeless body the following morning. I have always been too considerate, and even in planning to commit suicide I couldn't stop worrying about my family. Would they be afraid to live in the rooms where I had died? If they were, they would have nowhere to go—surely they would be helpless and friendless if I died in disgrace. Not only had I been branded a counterrevolutionary; I would be vilified for having "alienated myself from the people." No, killing myself at home was not an option.

The deed would have to be done elsewhere, which opened up a range of choices. Cheng, the Chinese Department's Party branch secretary, inspired me to consider the thick woods of the Western Hills. Lying there under the wide sky on a bed of pine needles with a stream warbling in the background might have been a poetic way to end one's life. But it was some distance from home, and I would get in trouble if any Red Guards caught me on the way. I considered finding a spot in Beijing's imperial Summer Palace, where the early twentieth-century scholar Wang Guowei had famously drowned himself in a lake. Not that I wanted to drown; I would prefer to find a cave, swallow a bottle of sleeping pills, and slip away quietly. But upon reflecting that I might startle the Summer Palace's many visitors, I decided that the Old Summer Palace, just across the road from home, was a better option. There were large beds of rushes in the park, and at the beginning of winter, they would be in full bloom. I would only have to lie down among the rushes and take my sleeping pills. It would be a quick, clean way to die. I was pleased with this plan. Ingenious, I thought to myself.

I was surprised that I felt so calm. I knew nothing of the psychology of suicide—after all, Qu Yuan had written about walking along the river where he was eventually to drown himself, but not about the actual drowning itself. I had thought that someone on the brink of suicide would be weeping hysterically, pacing up and down, plunged into inner turmoil. The fifth-century poet Jiang Yan wrote that "anyone who dies does so with bitterness and weeps inwardly." I could not fathom why I was still so serene.

To be sure, I was unsettled by the thought that I would be lying in the rushes in the Old Summer Palace the following day. Hardly anyone went there at this time of year, and it would take days for someone to discover my body, already decaying or perhaps torn apart by scavenging animals. Right now I was still in one piece, but I trembled to think what my dead body would look like when discovered. I imagined the announcements that New Beida would broadcast over and over again: "The counterrevolutionary Ji Xianlin has alienated himself from the people by committing suicide instead of facing his guilt! Ji Xianlin has committed suicide!" I knew all too well that the Jinggangshan broadcasts wouldn't hesitate to compete with New Beida in denouncing me.

But despite all this, I was determined to go ahead with my plan. I had made my decision and there was no going back. In what were to be the last few hours of my fifty-odd years, I thought of my elderly aunt, who had suffered through so much with me, my wife of four decades, my children, family, and few loyal friends. There were many people whose forgiveness I would have to ask for taking this step, and all I could say was: "See you on the other side!" I took my few bank deposit certificates and handed them to my wife and aunt without a word. "This is all you'll have to live on from now on, you poor things," I was thinking. "Please don't blame me for being selfish. I have no other choice." They seemed to understand me and didn't weep or become emotional. I gave no thought to making a will or disposing of my treasured books since these were my last moments with my family. Again, I was surprised by my calm.

I had suffered from insomnia for decades, and since I always lived frugally, I had a stash of Chinese and Western medicines in both pill and liquid form. I put them all in a small cloth bag, planning to swallow the pills first then wash them down with the syrups. If I climbed over the back wall, crossed a stream, then a road, I would be in the Old Summer Palace. Everything was ready, and I was about to step out of the door...

# AT THE ELEVENTH HOUR

BUT BEFORE I opened the door, someone rapped on it harshly; I knew immediately that it must be the Red Guards. Sure enough, three students barged in, their armbands glittering, ready to march me off to a struggle session like a lamb to the slaughter.

I knew I had no right to say anything. I stowed my pouch of sleeping pills away and followed the guards out meekly. My wife and aunt watched wordlessly as I was led away, aware that the violence of the struggle session could be fatal. Two Red Guards escorted me on either side, and one brought up the rear. "We won't tolerate your insolence any longer," they barked. "We'll get even with you today!" I was silent. I realized that the cruelty I had previously witnessed in struggle sessions was about to befall me. I wasn't a bystander any longer—I was about to become the star of the show. My thoughts were a blur, and yet it was no use being afraid. I wondered whether this was how being led to execution would feel. I would almost rather be beheaded or shot—at least the worst would be over in a single blow, a round of bullets, whereas now I didn't know how my persecutors planned to torment me or how long it would last.

On the way, I couldn't bring myself to look up or make eye contact with anyone. I wondered what other passersby thought of me. I thought of "Public Execution," the short story in which Lu Xun describes a criminal who can't hear what people are whispering as they point at him. I couldn't hear what anyone was saying about me either and wasn't sure I wanted to know.

Eventually we arrived at our destination, which I recognized from the tiles on the floor as the main student cafeteria—the largest indoor venue on campus. We went in through the back door, and I saw a row of other victims standing there, facing the wall like meditative Bodhidharmas. I dared not look directly at them, so I couldn't see who they were. But I could hear a few familiar voices. The crowd consisted of New Beida people; there would be no Jinggangshan supporters here. I waited. Suddenly, a slap rang out, but I felt nothing. Some other unlucky victim, then. Another slap rang out, and I felt my face burn. I was getting nervous. Then it was a heavy blow to my back, a well-aimed kick. It was only natural that New Beida should be hostile to me, since I had dared to oppose their leader, but some of my persecutors seemed to be motivated by sadism as well as revenge. Chinese sages have always stressed the superiority of man over beast. I find myself agreeing instead with Lu Xun, who pointed out that at least animals do not lecture their victims on why it is right that they be eaten. By contrast, think of man-eating humans and the excuses they invent. Beasts are more honest than the supporters of New Beida: They kill in order to eat.

But these reflections came later. At the time I was petrified, like a hog awaiting slaughter. I was nervous and agitated, disoriented but still alert. Facing the wall, I could feel my ears tingle as I braced myself for more blows. I knew this was only the start.

The show began. "Bring Ji Xianlin here!" they cried. Two Red Guards advanced toward me, twisting my arms behind my back and pushing my head down. They steered me into the leftmost corner of the stage. "Bend over!" I bent over. "Head down!" I lowered my head. But then I felt a blow to my back: "Lower!" I bent over further. A vicious kick: "Even lower!" Bending as far as I could, I wobbled and clutched my knees. More blows: "No holding your knees!" I held my arms out, all my weight shifting to my legs; I could barely stay balanced in the contorted position that I would later find out was the infamous airplane position. In the several minutes that the Red Guards had spent fine-tuning my posture, my legs were already exhausted. If I gave up and knelt down, I knew I would get a beating. I had to hold out.

Suddenly I heard someone making a speech from the podium. I couldn't see how many victims and Red Guards there were on the platform, or how big the crowd was, and I didn't dare look up. But slogans rang out, and the room swarmed with people. I couldn't hear the speech, but I was dimly aware that I was only a minor character, and the protagonist was an old cadre named Ge, who was a "Type 38 rifle," a Communist who had joined the party at the beginning of the Second World War. He had served as the president of Hebei University and the vice president as well as Party committee secretary of Peking University. He, too, was being attacked because he had opposed the Empress Dowager. I was relieved to find that I was playing a supporting role. Ge was probably positioned to my right, at the center of the stage, but I couldn't tell whether he was standing, sitting, kneeling, or holding the airplane position. I heard slaps, blows, kicks, and I could only imagine what he must be enduring. Perhaps someone was burning his skin with cigarettes.

I was in a precarious position. My legs could barely support the weight of my body. My head began to swim and I was drenched in sweat. But I gritted my teeth and told myself: "Don't give up! Think what would happen if you collapsed." Suddenly, a gob of spit landed on my left check. Unable to wipe it away, I gritted my teeth and began to count to a thousand, to make the time pass more quickly. It felt as though the entire cafeteria had gone silent, and I was the only person in it, the only person in the university, in Beijing, in all China.

Suddenly I became aware of the roar of slogans again. The session had ended. Before I had a chance to catch my breath, I was seized by the neck and arms, and herded onto an open-top truck. I realized that the show wasn't over, and that we were going to be publicly paraded. Again, I was flanked on either side by a Red Guard clutching me by each arm. I could see nothing. People in the crowd began to throw stones at me, hitting my face and body. I was aware of being kicked, punched, spat on, and yet I was unable to fight back. Despite having lived near campus for nearly twenty years, I couldn't tell where the truck was going. I felt like a sailboat lost at sea or a fox surrounded by hounds. The slogans were making me dizzy, and I gave myself up for lost.

Eventually someone—either a student or a worker—kicked me off the cart. I fell to the ground and was trying to get up when an elderly worker came up and punched me in the face, making my nose and mouth bleed. I knew this man. He wasn't worthy to be a member of the proletariat. He would later be nominated to welcome the troops of the 8341 Special Regiment on behalf of the workers of Peking University, a choice that horrified me—but that is another story. Right then, I panicked: My nose and mouth were full of blood. "Leave!" the man barked. I was free to go, and felt like a death row prisoner in the old novels receiving a pardon. I recovered somewhat, and realized that I had lost my hat. I also appeared to be wearing only one shoe, but I hobbled home anyway. My family was shocked to see me in such a state, but overjoyed that I had made it home alive.

That was the first struggle session I had experienced in my fifty-odd years. It made me feel just how cruel human beings could be to each other, but it also saved my life. If I could survive this, I decided, I had nothing more to fear. Then I realized how narrowly I had escaped death. If the Red Guards had arrived half an hour later, I would have already climbed the wall into the Old Summer Palace and taken my pills. In fact, if I had been a little less stubborn about airing my views, the New Beida leaders in my department wouldn't have decided I needed to be taken down a peg, and I would be lying dead among the rushes. I realized that being stubborn toward wicked people has its advantages; after all, I am only alive now because I was too stubborn before. It turned out that I could endure greater pain than I had realized. Was choosing to live a good idea or a rash one? Even today I don't know for sure. Either way, if I was going to live, I would have to be mentally prepared for many more struggle sessions.

I still wonder who invented the struggle session. It may well have been a collective invention, but if it could be patented, the inventor would deserve a prize for his idiocy as well as his genius. Struggle is very much a spectacle, but what purpose does it serve? In imperial times, judges pierced their victims' fingernails with bamboo picks or had them flogged or tortured on the rack in order to extract confessions. But there was no need to make the victims of the modern struggle session confess that they were capitalist-roaders or counterrevolutionary academic authorities since their crimes had already been broadcast via megaphones and enumerated on big-character posters. Perhaps the inventor of the struggle session was a purist, an aesthete pursuing art for art's sake, or struggle for struggle's sake. Perhaps he was a sadist. To have created the airplane position he must have been an inspired aeronautical engineer. It is terrifying to think that the struggle session was invented not by a beast but by a human being.

Having narrowly escaped suicide meant I was available to be struggled against again. My own department's sessions began several days later, and there I was the star of the show. The process was the same. A rap at the door and two Red Guards (one less than the previous time) wearing red armbands stormed in and hauled me off to the Foreign Languages Building. I faced the wall, unable to see anything, only hearing the loud clamor. There were two others facing the wall, but this time they played supporting roles while I was the protagonist. I felt proud that the session was running smoothly, the department so well organized. Suddenly there was a great shout: "Bring Ji Xianlin here!" I was only a few steps from the podium, but with four hands twisting my arms behind my back and a few more on my shoulders, those few steps took a long time as people crowded around me, their fists raining down on my body. Eventually, I was pushed onto a familiar stage. I had stood there many times as the head of the department; now I was a counterrevolutionary and prisoner. A woman led the crowd in chanting slogans. "Down with the counter-revolutionary Ji Xianlin!" she cried, the crowd then repeating it in response. I was called a variety of epithets like "the Kuomintang hanger-on," "the capitalist-roader," and so on. I seemed to have earned just about every counterrevolutionary title in existence.

Glancing at the table, I saw a kitchen knife, a basket of half-burned letters, and a photograph of Chiang Kai-shek and Soong Mei-ling with a red cross on it. I nearly fainted with dismay. I was as good as dead: This evidence of my so-called crimes could easily incite the crowds to tear me to shreds. But since there was no escape, all I could do was wait and see what would happen next.

After all the chanting, the chairperson read a long list of Mao's sayings—"Making revolution is not a dinner party," "Your enemy won't go down if you don't strike him down," and so on—either to inspire the crowd or perhaps to frighten the victims. When he had finished reading, another man made a passionate speech enumerating my crimes. It sounded like Wang, the student of Thai who had been part of the raid on my house. I was still holding the airplane position and my legs throbbed with pain. Although I had to concentrate on maintaining my balance and was barely listening, I could tell that the speech consisted of nothing but lies and slander. When Wang grew passionate, the audience broke into cries of "Down with Ji Xianlin!" There was a palpable sense of righteous anger in the room. Soon people circled around again to punch and kick me. I had heard some-one else being beaten while I played a supporting role, and now it was my turn. I wondered what I must have looked like, but I couldn't see my own bruises and wounds. Then someone heaved me off the floor and the crowd continued to beat me. I couldn't have held the airplane position even if I tried. I recognized Zheng, who studied Hindi; Gu, who studied Korean; and Wang, who studied Thai. Zheng was a fast talker and a trusted lieutenant of Nie's; Gu and Wang were strong young men. Setting them on a helpless old man like me was overkill—even a robust woman could have overpowered me. It was like slaughtering the proverbial chicken with the knife used to butcher an ox.

The struggle session went on and on. I must've made for a good show. Finally, when everyone had had their fill of struggle, I heard someone cry: "Take Ji Xianlin away!" I was marched out of the building as more blows rained down on me. The audience rushed out after me, ready to give me another thrashing. Eventually, a lecturer of Arabic named Luo said something that calmed them down. By the time I reached the Democracy Building, the crowds had given up their chase. Only then did I realize that I hurt all over, and my face was sticky with blood and sweat. I walked home, having survived yet another violent encounter.

# REFORM THROUGH LABOR BEGINS

THE PEAK SEASON for struggle sessions lasted from the winter of 1967 until the early spring of 1968, a period when there was one every few days. By then I had grown used to them, and I valued my life too much to consider suicide again. That was the first stage of our ordeal; in the second stage, from the early spring until May 3, 1968, we were also forced to perform hard labor.

When the season began, every department was organizing struggle sessions, and anything could serve as an excuse for struggling against someone. I, for instance, was often attacked for my work in the Peking University Union, which I was involved with for many years; the first official commendation I ever received was for union activity. When Beijing was liberated, I joined the Communist society for professors, which later combined with other staff organizations to form a union. It was said that the workers of Peking University were reluctant to form a union with intellectuals, since they considered themselves the vanguard of the proletariat, but that they were pressured from above to accept this arrangement. In any case, I was elected to various roles within the new union. During campaign season, I made the rounds of the university press, hospital, and various schools, canvassing votes like an American politician. I was full of optimism back then, and enjoyed working alongside my younger colleagues and

staying up all night to prepare the halls for our assemblies. I sometimes asked myself how intellectuals stood in relation to the workers,
the vanguard of the proletariat. I was once given the authoritative
explanation that intellectuals are not *workers* but that they belong to
the *working class*. Not being any good at Marxism-Leninism, I wondered how one could belong to the working class without being a
worker. But although I didn't understand this explanation, I accepted
it so as not to make waves in the delicate relationship between the
professors and workers. After Peking University was relocated away
from the city center in 1952, I continued to devote myself to union
work. Only three or four professors had ever been named chairman
of the University Union, and I was one of them.

Strangely, during the Cultural Revolution, my union record
counted against me instead of for me. The workers' logic must have
run as follows: The proletariat might have been generous enough to
permit a professor to join a workers' organization, but allowing him
to become a leader within it was a travesty. I would happily confess
to being a capitalist intellectual because I could see that I often possessed selfish bourgeois inclinations—not that the workers themselves were perfectly selfless. But I was baffled by the battle cry:
"Down with the capitalist intellectuals in power!" If an intellectual
became a professor, a department chair, a vice principal, or even a
union leader, he was not in power. The university administration,
run by Communist cadres, held all the real power. As far as I could
tell, they worked hard to implement Party policy thoroughly, and
didn't deserve to be denounced as capitalist-roaders. Now the intellectuals were facing similar accusations.

As soon as the students began to persecute me, the workers joined
in. They were all physically stronger and more revolutionary (that is,
more brutal) than the students. In their spare time, they all enjoyed
popular comedic art forms such as crosstalk, but since a struggle session made for better entertainment than a good evening of cross talk,

they would not miss an opportunity to organize one.[1] Sure enough, two workers soon pounded on our door to haul me off to a struggle session. They were both on bicycles, but since I didn't have one, they had to get off theirs and escort me like a foreign dignitary, one on either side of me. Unfortunately, I was in no mood to appreciate the honor.

The rumor was that the workers were going to struggle against all three professors who had each served, at one point or another, as chairman of the University Union. That would make for a rare spectacle, like watching the most famous singers of the time share a stage. Unfortunately, one of these professors had already been transferred to the Academy of Sciences, and the other couldn't be found, so they were left with me. Instead of just evading work, they thought up the idea of replacing the struggle session with an indoor procession held in a large hall so that more people could satisfy their curiosity by joining in the spectacle. I didn't dare look up or say anything, so I couldn't tell how many bystanders there were, but from the laughter and shouting, I could tell that the performance had attracted quite a crowd. The workers lived up to their reputation as men of deeds rather than words: Instead of making long speeches, they limited themselves to punching and kicking and pelting me with stones. I was relieved at not having to hold the airplane position.

But the furor over my union work would not end so quickly. The masses were constantly driven by the fear of missing out on something new, and next the Asia-Africa Institute decided it wanted a piece of the action. The institute had been established on the orders of the Ministry of Education before the start of the Cultural Revolution, and Lu Ping himself had asked me to serve as its nominal head. I had few responsibilities and hence no reason to quarrel with anyone at the institute—in fact, we got along quite well. But now that I was being attacked, they wanted a chance to demonstrate their own revolutionary fervor, even if it meant kicking someone who was already down. They hauled me off to a small room in the institute at the southern end of campus. I wasn't impressed. The slogans were half-hearted, there was no kicking or punching, and I barely held the airplane position at all. The speeches were 90 percent nonsense and 9 percent lies, with 1 percent remaining as a grain of truth. If I were grading struggle sessions, this one would fail—I couldn't give it any more than a 3 out of 10.

There were so many struggle sessions that it would have been biologically and psychologically impossible to keep track of them all. At one in my own department, I recall glimpsing members of both Jinggangshan and New Beida among the spokespeople. Although the two factions fought violently using spears and other improvised weapons, you could barely tell them apart. Both were extreme leftist groups that subscribed to ridiculous metaphysical principles, and both declared their loyalty to the Red Queen, Madame Mao. Now that they had found a common enemy in me, they were united in their hatred. The following words had been found in my confiscated diaries: "Jiang Qing gave New Beida a shot of morphine, and now they're acting cocky again." This was deemed highly disrespectful and altogether unforgivable. Having grown used to struggle sessions, I had become a more discerning participant. In this case, I noted that the spokespeople were not very clever and the speeches poor. Even from where I was, holding the airplane position, I couldn't help despising them. But watching the two factions come together to attack me also made me reflect that I myself had proved susceptible to partisanship, as demonstrated by that very line from my diaries. I was outraged to think that the faction that I had supported was now turning against me.

My mind wandered during these sessions, and I often thought back to my childhood in the countryside. Had I stayed there, I would still be half illiterate and working in the fields every day. My family only had about half an acre of land. Eventually I would have been classified as a peasant and qualified to reeducate intellectuals. It would have been a hard life but a carefree one. As the poet Su Shi wrote, "A man's troubles begin when he learns to read." As a university professor, I had enjoyed numerous honors, but now I was classified as a counterrevolutionary academic authority and struggled against every day. I regretted ever having left the village. The heavens had played a nasty trick on me.

But what's past is past, so I decided to find a concrete way of improving my lot. The most urgent of the various problems I faced at the time was the difficulty of maintaining the airplane position for several continuous hours. I concluded that what I needed most was physical exercise, or more specifically, an endurance training plan for my legs. If you collapsed during a struggle session, the organizers assumed that you were trying to cause trouble, which would automatically earn you a beating. But holding the position wasn't easy. After half an hour in the airplane position, I was often sore all over and drenched in sweat; before long, I would grow light-headed and sway slightly, my ears ringing. To keep myself going, I sometimes repeated a Mao saying to myself: "Make up your mind to fight without counting the costs, overcome all obstacles, and strive for victory!" Or in my case: "Make up your mind to ignore the pain, overcome all obstacles, and strive not to collapse!" This generally worked. As I persevered, the slogans and speeches began to sound faint and faraway, like thunder on distant hilltops.

I had survived many struggle sessions this way, but often to the point of nearly collapsing. I consequently decided to devote time each day to voluntarily holding an airplane position on the balcony, counting inwardly to measure the passing minutes, until my head reeled and I was drenched in sweat. This exercise regimen might seem ludicrous, but I can testify that it actually took place.

Standing on the balcony also allowed me to keep an eye on the road and see if any Red Guards were coming to harass me. I have always been an impatient person and consequently very punctual. Although I couldn't guarantee that a struggle session would finish on time, I didn't want one delayed on my account.

One winter day, while I was standing in my usual position on the balcony, I saw a few sparrows sitting motionless on a bamboo fence in the yard. All the trees were bare except for a couple of green pines. It was a scene worthy of a Chinese brush painting, and my eyes lit up to observe this gift of beauty from the gods. I immediately reflected on my incorrigible capitalist revisionist tendency to take bourgeois delight in things around me, even in such absurd circumstances.

When the Red Guards dragged me along the lake to the Foreign Languages Building or elsewhere to be struggled against, I often fantasized about running away. I thought of the turtles sunning themselves on floating logs in the lake. Despite being slow creatures, at the slightest sound they flipped themselves with startling agility into the water and disappeared in a ripple. I saw the ants beneath my feet and wished I could disappear into the grass like an ant or fly away like a bird. Human bodies were simply too big, too much of a hindrance to escape.

And even if I did escape, where would I go? Returning home to my village was a foolish idea. That had been tried before, and New Beida would simply send people to arrest the runaway and punish him more savagely. But where else could I go? Some suggested that I could stay with friends or with relatives, and at one point I collected ration coupons used for different parts in the country, so that I wouldn't starve while on the run. But I realized that all my fantasies of running away were far more dangerous than simply staying put, as unpleasant as it might be to live in daily fear of the Red Guards and struggle sessions.

One day, a New Beida leader in my department gave the order that we were all to report to *laogai*, which consisted of performing daily labor. I was tired of being trapped at home all day and welcomed anything that would break the tedium. From then on, N. and I reported for work every day. Only a year before, when N. was being struggled against, I was in the audience—now, unexpectedly, we had become comrades, both prisoners of the department we had jointly founded.

We began work every morning at eight, supervised by a worker. We went home at twelve and returned to work from two to six. There were innumerable tasks and different work sites. For a stretch we'd be given a different job each day. We worked silently, like a pair of oxen under the overseer's whip. The workers of Peking University had become white-collar overseers who did no work themselves. Since they were the vanguard of the proletariat, and I their prisoner, I kept my opinions to myself. But I realized that the Cultural Revolution was merely an elaborate excuse for workers to persecute intellectuals. Before Liberation, professors at the university were much better paid than the workers, and some of them must have been arrogant types who treated the workers badly. But after Liberation, the tide turned, and the revolution allowed a whole store of pent-up resentment to be released. During a struggle session, you could hear the palms of certain workers slapping the cheeks of professors. I understand that some workers may refute this depiction of them, but I am only being honest, in the spirit of seeking truth from facts.

I was supervised by one of these workers, and had to obey his orders while he stood and watched. I didn't mind hard work, although it meant I had less time for my endurance training regimen; plus I lived in constant fear that any department or unit could find out where I was working and drag me off to a struggle session if they pleased. Sometimes if I was sent back to work after a session, I would experience a rush of relief at not having to hold the airplane position—working was pleasant in comparison. I was an incorrigible bourgeois capitalist, constantly finding something to enjoy.

On the way to work and back, I stayed away from the main roads so as to avoid running into the gangs of Red Guards that roamed the streets with their spears and red armbands. Someone like me was obviously a blackguard: gloomy-looking, dressed in patched, tattered clothes, and covered in dust. We blackguards were like birds at which anyone was free to take potshots. In fact, punching or slapping us was a legitimate revolutionary act. Even children knew that we were bad guys they were allowed to spit at or pelt with small stones. A few of them would even toss white lime in the blackguards' eyes, which was extremely dangerous and could cause blindness. Since we couldn't retaliate, all we could do was run away. Once, an eight-year-old with a brick in his hand called to me: "Come here! Let me hit you!" I hurried away—not too quickly, so as not to give the child a fright. I had no desire to risk going blind. As if being stepped on and struggled against was not miserable enough, blindness would be the last straw.

Steering clear of the main roads, I used the narrow back lanes instead. At the time, there were many more back lanes, running behind old houses or along ditches, littered with piles of garbage and smelling of sewage. No one else used those lanes, and they became my favorite haunts. They were peaceful except for the occasional company of a stray cat or dog unacquainted with class struggle. Cats knew only that I was a human, and they feared all humans equally. Whereas on the streets I would hurry along, eyes turned to the ground, here I could look up at the sky and enjoy my stroll, loitering as long as I pleased. These lanes were made for blackguards like me.

One day, at a work site where we were tasked with tearing down a bamboo stand, I stepped on a loose nail lying on the floor. The one-inch nail pierced through my thin shoe into the center of my foot. I felt a searing pain, and my foot wouldn't stop bleeding. "You people are such useless idiots!" the overseer said. I knew that by "you people" he meant "you professors," and braced myself for being slapped, but all he said was "Get lost!" I hurried away. Barely able to walk, I somehow made my way home, dragging my wounded leg behind my healthy one. I couldn't go to the hospital, which was controlled by the very members of New Beida I was trying to avoid. My aunt and wife were shocked to see me, but they disinfected my wound with hot water, put some antiseptic on it, and bandaged it. I had to go back to work in the afternoon, for not only would I be in trouble but the worker overseeing me might get in trouble himself. Whereas the Communists had insisted on treating captured Kuomintang soldiers in a "revolutionary humanitarian" way, the same standards didn't apply to us subhuman blackguards.

By this point, the two factions were getting into armed skirmishes. They had each started manufacturing weapons and assembling a small army. The ruling faction could afford to buy expensive steel rods and turn them into spears. Jinggangshan was less well funded, but they did their best too.

Each of the two factions took over several blocks on campus, guarding them like castles, and skirmishes broke out regularly. I never witnessed a battle, but I was once ordered to clear a field that had been the site of a fight. All the glass in the nearby building had been broken, and there were stones and bricks lying everywhere— these, too, had been used by both sides as weapons. But when I looked up, I couldn't help smiling at the sight of a string of tattered shoes hanging from one of the windows, another reference to one of Nie's nicknames. These grown-up children had turned the armed struggle between the two factions into a joke. It was the first time I had smiled in a long time.

Since both groups considered me their common enemy, I made sure to stay away from the actual fighting. No one who saw me would hesitate to attack me—and since I had escaped with my life thus far, I meant to stay alive. I wanted neither to kill myself nor to be killed. I wanted to live.

# THE GREAT STRUGGLE SESSION

AS THE DAYS passed, I continued to live in constant dread. Wherever I was, whether at home or at work, I could be dragged off to a struggle session in a flash. No matter how remote my work site, if I saw people wearing red armbands coming toward us from a distance, I knew what that meant. I would have to follow them as unquestioningly as if I were an ox. I had perfected the airplane position, and there was no need for the guards to correct my posture with blows. My endurance training had paid off, which meant that struggle sessions were still a little uncomfortable but didn't make my legs too sore. I had never paid much attention to the habitual political slogans and outright lies in all those so-called speeches, and now I simply ignored them. In any case, struggle sessions were a temporary reprieve from having to work. With the practical experience I had accumulated, I could have earned a certificate in surviving struggle sessions.

Sometimes the Red Guards didn't bring me to a struggle session but to an interrogation. These also took place in the Foreign Languages Building, though for reasons I never discovered, the location changed constantly. When we entered the room, the various New Beida leaders in my department would be sitting unsmiling in a row, like judges in court. I was expecting to be made to hold the airplane position, but they permitted me to stand in front of them. Like the servile eunuch Jia Gui, who refused to sit in the emperor's presence, I felt uneasy about being allowed to meet my interrogators' gaze. Although being uncooperative had once saved my life, I was now more cooperative, since I could tell that being stubborn served no purpose. The interrogations were usually about phrases culled from the millions of words in my diaries. They were always taken out of context and deliberately misread, which meant that the accusations were absurd. I had to suppress my anger, since I was compelled to respond. The feeling of having to bite my tongue constantly was maddening. Sometimes I thought I would prefer holding the airplane position and getting slapped in the face to having to listen to such nonsense—from the mountain you're standing on, the next mountain always seems taller.

All my interrogators were either students in my department or lecturers I had hired. I didn't subscribe to the old-fashioned notion that they were indebted to me and owed me respect, and I knew they were blinded by factionalism. But there were a few individuals who were especially vicious toward me. One of them, a Korean language instructor, appeared to be currying favor with the Empress Dowager by being spiteful toward me; another, an Indonesian language instructor who used to be very polite to me, was in fact hiding the skeletons in his own closet. He had taken part in anti-Soviet demonstrations before 1949, and now he was trying to make up for his past by persecuting me. His past was uncovered, and he committed suicide the capitalist way.

I felt especially bad for a certain Arabic language instructor. He was an honest man who bore no grudge against me. New Beida gave him the lowly assignment of reading my diaries. I knew better than anyone what a mind-numbing and thankless task that was. Taken out of context, nearly any phrase could serve as an excuse to struggle against me, but actually reading through that mountain of papers and diaries would require real patience. Even I had no desire to re-read my own diaries. But this man—I dare not classify myself as his comrade—actually stayed up all night going through my jottings and provided the New Beida leaders with much fodder for their interrogations. If Ji Xianlin were a worthwhile subject of study, "Ji-ology" might have been a profitable use of time. As it was, he had only wasted his efforts, which could have been put to better use reading Arabic literature or writing a master's thesis. I felt sorry for him, but there was nothing I could do about it.

The interrogations sometimes grew heated, but no one raised a finger against me during these gatherings, for which I was grateful. Nonetheless, I was growing tired of the constant cycle of hard labor, struggle sessions, and interrogations. Everyone around me treated me as an enemy, and one woman in our building tried persuading my wife and aunt to disown me, to which my wife replied, "We'd starve without him!" I started dreaming of a savior who would take pity on me and come to the rescue of an innocent man. Never having put my trust in any god, buddha, or bodhisattva, I turned instead to the Great Leader. At night, after long days of work and struggle sessions, I would sit up writing letters to Chairman Mao, hoping against hope for a miracle. People were saying that "the Cultural Revolution will take place once every eight years and last eight years each time," but I dreamed that the revolution would come to an end and that I would eventually be rehabilitated. As Du Fu's famous poem goes, "The traveler climbing a tall tower to gaze at flowers is overwhelmed by grief." My hopes were in vain: The cycle went on as before.

There was more trouble at home. The woman who had urged my family to disown me was pressing me to remove some furniture we had stored in her rooms, including a large sofa and an antique redwood table said to be the only one of its kind in Beijing. We only had two rooms left: a larger room we used for storage and a small room we lived in. The furniture wouldn't fit in the bike storage room, which had been wrecked by the Red Guards. I still didn't have the heart to clear up what was left of my books there, until a lecturer who lived downstairs put up a notice demanding that I remove the books and store them elsewhere. All my friends avoided me like the plague. To whom could I go for help? I felt like Xiang Yu on the banks of the Wu River, surrounded by enemy troops on all sides. I had already decided not to kill myself, but I didn't know how to go on living.

Things would only get worse. I labored all that spring. The flowers on campus bloomed heedless of the revolution taking place around them, but I might as well have been color-blind—they all looked gray to me. Chinese tradition holds that plans for the year ahead are best made in the spring, and the leaders of New Beida accordingly hatched a new plan for tormenting their victims. They may not all have been genuine revolutionaries, but many were genuine sadists who were finally able to give their cruelty full rein. During the Cultural Revolution, their sadistic instincts were, as it were, "liberated." I should point out that only a fraction of Peking University's several thousand workers and tens of thousands of students took part in persecuting the intellectuals. All of the factional members were good-for-nothings and lazy rascals who had found a perfect excuse to cause trouble.

On May 4, 1968, the anniversary of the May Fourth Movement, we convicts were marched from our homes to the coal plant. Everyone knew that the coal plant was run by a gang of workers who supported the Empress Dowager. They were brawny men who could easily lift whole sacks of coal, and we intellectual types were no match for them. They looked like the legendary outlaws in *The Water Margin* and had the strength to match, as anyone who had been beaten by them could attest.[1] The blackguards who had spent time working at the coal plant spoke of it with fear in their eyes, as if it were Zhazidong Prison, the coal mine that was turned into a Kuomintang camp for political prisoners.

73

Once we arrived at the plant, I noticed that only a subset of the blackguards had been selected for this honorable session. Among us were Lu Ping and Peng Peiyun, both mentioned by name in the first Marxist-Leninist poster. Wooden boards bearing our names and weighing at least a dozen pounds each were hung around our necks. We were ordered to sit on the floor and did so silently. Anticipating a long struggle session, I asked for permission to go to the outhouse, which was some distance away. I stumbled there and back as fast as I could with the wooden board hanging around my neck and joined the other counterrevolutionaries sitting on the floor, my heart pounding as if I were waiting to be executed.

Finally someone cried out that we were to be taken away and a crowd of men engulfed us. Each prisoner was held by two men who twisted our arms behind our backs and gripped us by the shoulders. They led us to a place I vaguely recognized as the No. 3 Student Cafeteria. We entered from the door on the left, and were lined up and forced into the airplane position. Since there was no podium, the speakers stood in a row behind a long table. I glanced to my right and saw Peng Peiyun, but I couldn't make out any of the other counterrevolutionaries. As usual, there were deafening cries of "Down with So-and-so!," followed by Mao's sayings and interminable speeches. I had become so numb to these proceedings that I could barely hear a word they said. I was desperate for the session to end. I couldn't see my wrist and probably wasn't wearing a watch anyway, so I counted silently: one, two, three, four, five, six, seven, eight, and reached several thousand. The shouting continued, but my legs turned to lead and I started to see stars. I stopped counting. To my right, I could see a small puddle of sweat dripping from Peng's brow onto the ground. I couldn't see the ground beneath my own feet, but the wooden board seemed to be growing heavier, and the steel wire was cutting into my flesh.

I was barely conscious when someone said: "Take them all away!"

The ceremony was over. But as before, the worst was yet to come. My arms were twisted behind my back and at least three people gripped my shoulders; I could barely lift my head or stand up straight. I was marched out of No. 3 Student Cafeteria onto the streets full of jostling crowds. The bystanders made a racket that sounded like a chorus of cicadas on a summer night. This parade went much faster than the previous march. Having just spent hours holding the airplane position and wearing a wooden board, I could barely walk. Instead of helping me along, the young men on either side of me dragged me like a dead dog through the streets. I quickly wore through my battered shoes and socks, which meant that my exposed feet trailed along the ground. I was insensible to the pain. I knew that I was being pelted with small rocks, but I was only dimly aware of the journey to the main cafeteria and back. Then I was flung on the ground. When I recovered my senses, I realized I was lying outside the coal plant.

This was the most draining struggle session I had experienced. I was lying on the ground—my ears ringing, heart beating rapidly—too faint to get up. I became aware of blood trickling from my toes. The crowds had gone to dinner, and I looked up to see two of the other victims, Zhang Xueshu and Wang Enyong. Being younger and stronger than me, they helped me up and brought me home. I will never forget their kindness.

# TAIPING VILLAGE

AFTER THAT DEBILITATING struggle session, I longed for a few days' rest—I simply couldn't endure it anymore. But the Red Guards knew that iron must be hammered into shape while still hot, and they had already planned our next ordeal. The following day, more than a hundred of us received the order to pack our belongings and report to the coal plant. I despaired at the thought of new torments. As I was lugging my trunk along a lakeside path, I ran into an economics professor named Hu. Having earlier been labeled a capitalist-roader, he had not been rehabilitated and was looking despondent. I envied him enormously for not having been summoned to the coal plant.

The following day, I hurried nervously into the plant. The place itself struck fear into all the blackguards. With the previous day's events fresh in my mind, I was terrified. I was made to stand outside beneath a wooden board, bent at the waist. I was mentally prepared to be punched or slapped. But I waited, and nothing happened. I began to worry about what new tricks the guards had up their sleeves. I would've preferred if they slapped and kicked us as usual.

We were told to line up two by two, and someone who looked like a New Beida student began to lecture us, brandishing a spear. "You turtles, listen up. None of you will ever be rehabilitated!" We could actually hear him, since we didn't have to focus on holding the airplane position. "My spear is not a vegetarian spear!" he said. I believed him, especially since deaths at the time went unprosecuted, and New Beida had already been responsible for a few deaths. Killing a blackguard was like squashing a fly; no one paid any notice. As he spoke, his companions hustled a handful of blackguards at random out of the group, beat them savagely on the sidelines, and then forced them to return to their original places. Their tactic was to make an example of a few people in order to terrorize us all. To my relief, I was spared.

We were rounded up onto a couple of pickup trucks. It was about an hour's drive to the Peking University campus, known as "No. 200" because the original blueprint for the building project had supposedly been coded #60-200. The campus was not far from the Ming dynasty imperial tombs outside the city, and from there it was a five-kilometer walk to our eventual destination, Taiping Village. Unexpectedly, although everyone else had to walk, the guards had been thoughtful and kind enough to arrange for me and a few other older prisoners to be taken there by car.

We would be living in a row of derelict huts, four convicts to a hut. The doors and windows were nearly all broken, everything was coated in a thick layer of dust, and the beds were covered with mud. As blackguards, we had no right to demand any better. I was assigned to share a hut with N., the elderly professor of Eastern languages, as well as Professor Zhao from the Politics Department whom I knew well. He had progressed from being labeled a capitalist-roader in the earliest stage of the movement to being a counterrevolutionary academic authority. Even though we were old acquaintances, we sat there stiffly, none of us daring to speak or smile. To use a Marxist term, we had been "alienated" from our own humanity.

We had traveled all day in hot weather, and I had not had a drop to drink since that morning. My thirst was overwhelming.

*Water water water...*

I would have drunk anything: river water, lake water, sea water, ditch water...There seemed no greater happiness known to man than that of quenching one's thirst. I vowed that the moment I was freed, the first thing I would do was drink a tall glass of water, or better yet, an ice-cold beer. *Water water water*, I thought. I was suddenly reminded of a line from *The Rime of the Ancient Mariner*: "Water, water, everywhere, and not a drop to drink." But there wasn't a drop of water to be seen anywhere in the desert surrounding us.

The huts lay at the foot of Yan Mountain, with the peak to our north and the fields stretching out to our south. Even Taiping Village itself was some distance away. Although we were completely isolated, the guards insisted on carrying their spears at all times, as if they were truly afraid that we would plan an uprising—we, a group of aging intellectuals who probably couldn't kill a chicken if we tried. Of course, we had neither the strength nor the courage to revolt. We would have counted ourselves lucky merely to survive. Nonetheless, I was amused that the guards saw the need to take such precautions. The rules were especially strict at night. You couldn't even use the outhouse without requesting permission or you risked being speared to death. We had all been duly warned. One night, wanting to relieve myself, I tiptoed out into the moonlit night and cried "Reporting!" into the nighttime silence. Then I waited until an invisible spear-wielding voice replied, "Go!"

The educational component of *laogai* consisted entirely of hard labor, and on this occasion, our job was to plant sweet potato seedlings, which would have been light work if I wasn't in pain from the previous day's beating. I knelt stiffly on the ground and began to work steadily. Before long, someone thumped me on the head with a cudgel, and I looked up to see a guard with a spear in one hand and a cudgel in the other. "Ji Xianlin! Be careful or you'll get it!" he shouted. I didn't want to get it, so I bent over and worked so hard that my fingertips began to bleed.

It was the beginning of summer, the peach and apricot blossoms had already wilted, the woods were green, and thousands of tiny flowers carpeted the plains beneath the mountains. I was working furiously and had no time to admire the view. But as I glanced at the woods, these words came into my mind:

While planting seedlings beneath Yan Mountain,
Disaffectedly, I catch sight of the green forest.

They were an echo of two lines by the fourth-century poet Tao Yuanming:

While picking chrysanthemums by the eastern fence,
Tranquilly, I catch sight of South Mountain.

Nature may be indifferent to "class struggle" and the squandering of human talent described by the poet Qu Yuan as "golden bells being smashed, while clay pots clang loudly," but human beings cannot remain indifferent to our own circumstances.

After only a few days of work, my body collapsed under the physical and mental strain, exacerbated by injuries from the struggle sessions. My testicles became so swollen that I couldn't even stand up or close my legs, let alone walk anywhere. Planting seedlings was out of the question. I was unable to drag myself out of the hut for lunch, so the guards took pity on me and ordered N. to bring me food. But work was mandatory, so they ordered me to pick up stones and bricks in the yard and toss them over the fence. I spread my legs, crawled toward the bricks, made a heap of them, and crawled toward the fence to hurl them over. The other blackguards had gone to work in the fields, and only a few watchmen remained at the huts. The huts and yard, field and forest were blanketed by a silence that city dwellers cannot imagine. As I crawled about wordlessly, I couldn't help weeping.

Two days later, seeing that my condition showed no signs of im-
provement, the guards ordered me to report to the military clinic on
campus at No. 200, and warned me to declare that I was a blackguard. I spread my legs gingerly and crawled out onto the road like a
snail. On the way, I met a fellow blackguard Ma Shiyi. He was pushing a cart to Changping to buy vegetables. He offered to take me to
No. 200 on his cart, but I didn't dare accept. To this day I have not
forgotten his generosity.

It took me two hours to crawl to the military clinic at No. 200.
There was a doctor in military uniform on duty, and his bright red
badge awakened a glimmer of hope. When he saw me, he immediately rose to help. "Doctor, I am a blackguard," I declared, following
orders. The doctor's face darkened instantly, and he refused to touch
me, as if I had the plague. "Get out of here!" he said quickly. I was
hoping he would at least examine my swollen testicles and give me
some painkillers. The brightness of his red badge appeared to fade
suddenly. But there was nothing I could do except crawl back to
the hut.

Human beings have a remarkable capacity for enduring pain. A
few days later, without any medication, the swelling subsided and I
could return to work on the hillside. All the potato seedlings had been
planted, so the Red Guards ordered N. and me to fill in the potholes
beneath the peach trees. We were a small team overseen by a single
man, a lecturer in Arabic studies from our department. He used to be
our student, but now that he was in charge, he lorded over us fiercely
with his spear, like one of the Four Great Buddhist Kings. The peach
grove was even quieter and more beautiful than the farm, but I was
not in the mood to enjoy it.

Our living conditions were primitive. We ate on the beach of a dry
lake at the foot of the mountains, near a cluster of houses that were
cleaner than our huts, each containing a kitchen. The Red Guards ate
separately at a table indoors, while we ate our coarse rice and corn-

meal buns in the yard or under the trees. Even boiled vegetables or deep-fried bread were luxuries beyond our reach.

Although we did nothing but eat, work, and sleep, there was one great reprieve: We were safe from the constant threat of struggle sessions, the dreaded airplane position, and the interminable nonsense of political speeches. I think all of us would have been happy to stay in the village.

# BUILDING OUR OWN PRISON

BUT IT WASN'T to be.

If we had been better acquainted with the Red Guards' whims, we would have known more was coming.

I never discovered why we were sent to Taiping Village. Whatever the reason, after only a few weeks we were ordered to return to campus. The car dropped us off at the coal plant, and the same New Beida student who had previously given us a long lecture, lectured us again. I had no idea what to expect next, but the following day, we were summoned to the single-story buildings between the Foreign Languages Building and the Democracy Building and told to construct the cowsheds in which we would eventually be imprisoned. We were literally to make our beds and then sleep in them.

I knew these small buildings well. I walked past them every day on my way to work and had taught classes in them. The sun burned down through the thin roofs in the summer, and the broken windows offered no protection against the wind. The brick-tiled floors were damp and moldy. Even the installation of stoves wouldn't keep these buildings warm. They were slowly falling apart.

But New Beida's leaders had evidently decided that this would be our prison. The Democracy Building would be the eastern boundary of the cowsheds, the Foreign Languages Building would be the southern boundary, and we were to erect reed mats as temporary walls on the northern and western sides. Reed mats stretching across the gap between the two buildings served as "doors." Twenty blackguards were allocated to each building, with separate ones for men and women, giving us all barely enough space to lie on the floor. Because the buildings had long since fallen into disuse, the floors were unbearably dank. Eventually it was announced that the Empress Dowager had arranged for us to receive a truckload of wooden planks to be laid on the floors. Of course the Red Guards couldn't be expected to live in the buildings. They established their headquarters in the Democracy Building, arranging offices and some living quarters. They continued to take extensive precautions against us. During the day, the back doors of the Democracy Building that faced the cowshed were left open, with defensive measures that included plenty of barbed wire and spears. At night, the doors were locked to prevent prisoner break-ins. A shed built of reed mats was built next to the women's quarters. It was originally called the transfer room, and was later renamed the interrogation room to make it sound more revolutionary. Many prisoners were questioned there and severely beaten. A larger area was converted into an open-air cafeteria for the blackguards.

The yard was full of potholes and overgrown with weeds. It hadn't been used in a long time, and would now have to be cleaned up so we could move in. The men were divided into cleaning teams, while the women and elderly were assigned a variety of other jobs. Although the yard was bustling with activity, all the prisoners worked in complete silence—an entire army of forced laborers.

I was assigned to a team responsible for constructing a barrier around the cowshed. We dug a large trench to the east of what is now the Archaeology Building, planted wooden stakes in it, and built a makeshift frame by hammering long planks across the tops of the stakes. Finally, we nailed reed mats onto the planks, creating a wall that was more than ten feet high. Only days ago, this had been a passageway, and now it was completely sealed off and impassable.

After the barrier had been built, I was reassigned to work in the interrogation room, where my task was to level the ground with spades and wooden rods. We were all terrified of being punished. No one protested and everyone worked hard. Here the guards carried cudgels instead of the spears they had brandished in Taiping Village, perhaps because they felt safer now that they were back at New Beida's home base. But we were acutely aware that their spears lay within immediate reach inside the Democracy Building, and that they were, as we had been warned, "not vegetarian."

There was a professor from the Western Languages Department, probably in his seventies, who often walked around with a dazed look in his eyes. He hadn't been sent to Taiping Village, nor had he been targeted in a struggle session, so he didn't retain the same terror of the guards that we felt. But his misfortune revealed that our own fears were not misplaced. One day, he rested for a moment while working and allowed his spade to stop moving. Little did he know that a guard was standing right behind him with a cudgel. The guard struck him heavily on the back, and only then did he come to attention and begin swinging his spade again. After this interlude, a symphony of spades hitting the ground could be heard throughout the interrogation room.

Finally, when the cowshed was ready, the words "Down with all cow devils!" were painted in large white characters on a south-facing wall as a finishing touch. The slogan was more terrifying than a hundred lectures by students wielding spears. Each character was taller than a person, and I privately noted that the brush calligraphy was some of the best I had ever seen. Indeed, writing big-character posters gave our students a chance to practice their calligraphy, beating people up allowed them to build their muscles, giving speeches in struggle sessions made them better liars, and getting into fights made them bolder. No effort expended during the Cultural Revolution was entirely wasted.

Lu Xun was right when he said that China is a country of the written word. Centuries ago, during the Han dynasty, people wrote sayings like "Ill dreams at night, safe in daylight" over their doorways to guard against bad luck triggered by a nightmare. Proverbs like this are everywhere in China. Ghosts are said to fear certain sayings, such as "Stones from Mount Tai ward off evil." Socialist China likewise has not evolved beyond the power of the written word. We plaster the slogan "Serve the people!" everywhere, as if merely saying so means that the people have already been served. Similarly, the words "Down with all cow devils!" above our heads proved that we cow devils had already been struggled against and defeated. This was a simple, elegant, and eminently Chinese solution.

From then on, we inmates lived in the shadow of those words.

# IN THE COWSHED (1)

WE WERE ABOUT to be herded into the prison we had built with our own hands. As the novelist Hu Feng said, "There is life to be lived everywhere"—even in the cowshed.[1] But finding a way to talk about living life in the cowshed is not so easy. I finally decided on the technique, much beloved by Chinese historians, of coming up with a theory as an organizing principle for my story. My theory has no basis in the academic literature, and it wouldn't stand up to professional scrutiny. It is based purely on fieldwork, but I am nonetheless convinced of its truth.

I propose the Law of Maximum Torment: that everything the Red Guards did, no matter where their loyalties lay or what Party line they were defending, was calculated to inflict maximum pain on their victims. Their psychological and intellectual motivations I've already discussed above. Regardless of whether they were raiding intellectuals' houses or reforming them through labor, their chief aim was to inflict pain. At the outset, they were limited to primitive methods they had learned from historical novels about feudal society. Even cavemen must have known how to slap and kick their victims. But the Red Guards were bright students, and they were good at swapping tips and learning from each other. They soon invented more sophisticated methods of tormenting their victims. Just as military technology develops quickly during wartime, torture techniques developed quickly during the Cultural Revolution. When one campus invented a new technique, it often spread like lightning across the country; the Red Guards at Peking University, for instance, could have patented the practice of hanging wooden boards around their victims' necks. During the Cultural Revolution, Red Guards nationwide collaborated to design a methodology of torture so comprehensive that it ought to be preserved for future use. So much for my theory—an account of how it was put into practice in the cowshed follows.

## PROPER NAMES

As Confucius said, "Everything must have its proper name, or else speech isn't in accordance with the nature of things." To begin with, the revolutionaries would have to decide what the cowshed's inmates were called. We had been called "blackguards" or "turtles," but those were mere insults. Officially we were called "counterrevolutionaries," but for some reason that didn't catch on. None of the other names lasted very long, so even after the cowshed had been built, there was no consensus on our official designation. When we first moved in, there was a notice in each building titled "Rules for Persons Undergoing Reform Through Labor." The tone was severe and the rules were detailed. The elegant handwriting suggested that the writer was a man of letters. No one was asserting the rule of law at that stage, and yet our very own Red Guards had managed to draw up rules resembling actual laws that earned their victims' grudging respect.

But they had made one mistake. The "Rules for Persons Undergoing Reform Through Labor" disappeared from the walls within a couple of days, to be replaced by "Rules for Reform-Through-Labor

Convicts." Much better! Now that we had been informed of our status as convicts, we would accept our legal position and resign ourselves to living in terror with no hope of ever being rehabilitated. I wrote this little ditty:

The prison has been built;
A name has been found.
The convicts know their guilt;
All's right, peace abounds.

## THE BUILDINGS

The blackguards lived in three badly built buildings that were intended to be temporary structures, little sturdier than bamboo stands. When there weren't enough empty classrooms, we used to hold classes in these buildings. But now that classes had been suspended for two years while students all over China made revolution, the buildings had been abandoned. They were damp, musty, cobwebby places, full of rats, lizards, caterpillars, cockroaches, scorpions, and various other creatures; in short, they were unfit shelters for human beings. Then again, as convicts, not human beings, we had no right to expect much more than a roof over our heads.

At first we slept on bamboo mats covering the dank brick floors. The thin layer of hay beneath the mats was no use against the dampness. By day the buildings were full of flies; by night they were full of mosquitoes. We were covered from head to toe with insect bites. Eventually we were given planks on which to lay our mats and rags drenched with pesticide to guard against mosquitoes. We were grateful for these humanitarian measures.

No one seemed to know why our numbers had increased—there were far more of us here than there had been in Taiping Village. But

Very Important Prisoners such as Lu Ping were not to be seen in the cowshed and must have been imprisoned elsewhere. Some of the new prisoners I had seen at struggle sessions, but others, new targets of the progressing "class struggle," I had never seen before. New faces continued to join us throughout our stay, and the cowshed family grew steadily.

## THE DAILY ROUTINE

Officially, the constitution of the cowshed was the "Rules for Reform-Through-Labor Convicts," but it was liberally supplemented with unwritten laws. Without a legislative body such as the Council of Convicts, our overseers could speak laws into being unhindered by democratic formalities; their every word was accepted as truth.

Regulated thus by laws both written and unwritten, life in the cowshed was orderly. Waking any earlier or later than the regulation time of 6 a.m. was prohibited. At the clanging of a bell, we got dressed and jogged around the yard. The guards barked their orders from the center of the yard, which they must have considered a position of safety since they rarely carried spears during the morning jog.

Why did the Red Guards institute a daily exercise regimen? Inmates of the cowshed didn't lack exercise; our lives as *laogai* convicts consisted of nothing but hard labor, and we weren't even permitted to read for pleasure. The verdicts on our cases were irreversible, and death would have been too good for us, so there was no need to keep fit. No, the morning jog was motivated by the Law of Maximum Torment, the principle that everything in the cowshed had to be organized to inflict maximum pain on its inmates. Its sole purpose was to ensure that we had worn ourselves out before even beginning the day's labor.

After our jog, we washed ourselves at the taps in the yard before trudging to the cafeteria for breakfast, staring at the ground the whole way. There were more than a hundred of us, and not one dared to risk a kick or blow to the back by breaching the unwritten rule against looking up. At the cafeteria, we could only buy steamed corn-meal buns or pickles, luxuries such as scallion pancakes being forbidden to convicts. In any case, our allowance was sixteen yuan and fifty cents, with another twelve yuan and fifty cents for dependents—we were barely scraping by, and even if we had been allowed other types of food, I wouldn't have been able to afford them.

The cafeteria had tables and chairs, but they were meant for human beings, not for us. Inmates ate outside, squatting under the trees or on the steps. At meals, we eyed the meat dishes hungrily while chewing on our cucumbers or boiled vegetables, a diet that left us without a drop of oil in our stomachs after a day of hard labor. We barely had enough ration coupons to buy cornmeal buns. I had gone hungry during the war in Germany and during the three years of famine around 1960, but this experience differed fundamentally from the others: In the cowshed, starving was augmented by physical exertion and the constant threat of a beating; by comparison, those earlier times of starvation seemed like bliss.

We returned to the cowshed after breakfast, waiting like oxen to be given our tasks for the day. None of the university's janitors and workers did any labor; they had all become overseers or guards. When there was a dirty or tiring job to be done, they could simply come to the cowshed and request manpower, just as the leader of a village production team might request a team of oxen. When all the jobs had been assigned, the workers would relax and give orders from the sidelines, looking smug.

Before beginning the day's labor, every convict had to copy the Mao saying of the day from a blackboard that hung from a branch. The sayings were often quite long. But it was crucial to learn them by heart, because no matter where you were working and what you were doing, a guard could order you to recite the saying for the day at any time. Get one word wrong, and you risked being slapped in the face, at the very least. If you were called to the office, you would cry "Reporting!" and stand there stiffly, staring at the floor. When a guard recited the first phrase of any quotation from Chairman Mao, that would be your cue to complete the sentence unless you wanted a beating. One old physics professor's brain seemed to have become sluggish with age. Stuffed to the brim with mathematical formulae, it had no room for anything else—not even the Great Leader's words. As a result, I often saw his cheeks swollen, his eyes puffy with bruises.

Perhaps our overseers thought that ordinary methods used to reform criminal elements wouldn't work on us and decided to try Jesuit catechizing techniques instead. But although memorization is said to be extraordinarily effective as an educational technique, it seemed to have little effect on me. It is more likely that the Maoist catechizing served no rehabilitative purpose and was instead motivated by the Law of Maximum Torment. After all, our overseers themselves didn't believe in the educational power of Mao's words. They could barely recite the sayings. When a guard began to recite a quotation from Chairman Mao, I sometimes blundered in my haste to complete it, but the guards rarely noticed. I could get away with a mistake or two, since at least I wasn't stupid enough to cause trouble for myself by admitting my own errors and making the guards lose face.

While working, we learned the sayings by heart, our physical and mental capacities alike stretched to breaking point.

One of my longest assignments was at the Northern Materials Factory. All the workers there belonged to New Beida and supported the Empress Dowager. They were particularly hostile to me since I was known to be a Jinggangshan man. Our first task was to transport fire-resistant bricks from inside the factory to a stockpile next to the pond. The bricks had to be stacked with extreme caution, since a tower of bricks could crush a man to death if it collapsed. All the inmates knew this and we worked very carefully.

After all the bricks had been moved to the stockpile, we were assigned to pull nails out of old planks. This was light work, and we were even permitted the luxury of sitting on wooden stools as we worked. Next, we were reassigned to shovel construction sand piled outside the factory. I must have spent several weeks in the Northern Materials Factory. I don't know what tasks the other inmates were given, since not all of them worked there.

I was later transferred from the factory to a job piling up coal in the student dorms. Truckers considered their job done once they had unloaded the coal and dumped it on the ground. Our job was to gather the scattered coal into baskets and pile it into heaps so it would take up less space. It was the height of summer, and this was dirty, exhausting work. We clambered up the heap repeatedly, two old men hauling a basket of coal that could weigh up to 130 pounds. In strong wind, our faces and clothes were coated in a film of coal dust. As professors, we would never have set foot here, but times had changed, and we had to change with them. It was impossible to avoid the grime. My partner was an old Muslim comrade who had risked his life working in the underground Communist Party at Yenching University, which became a part of Peking University. One day, when the overseer's back was turned, he whispered to me under his breath, "Our fates have been sealed. We'll live out our lives in labor camps in some remote province." To the extent that I thought about the future, I probably thought the same.

I was assigned many other tasks, such as weeding or doing repairs, and will refrain from listing them all here. I was part of a large contingent of blackguards that carried rocks and plowed paddy fields on the side of campus near the present site of Shaoyuan Building. On another occasion, I was assigned, along with a professor of Western languages, to help a plumber fix the underground piping outside the east wall of Block 35 dorm. The plumber did all the work himself, occasionally asking us to pass him his hammers or carry sacks of sand. He never smiled or said a word, nor did he shout at us. I was unbelievably grateful for this reprieve. In later years, when I saw him riding through campus on his bike, I often found my eyes following his silhouette as it receded from sight.

The life of a *laogai* convict consisted chiefly of physical labor. The guards' gaze was inescapable, both during and after working hours. But because of the unwritten rule that inmates were not to lift their eyes from the ground, an inmate might not realize that he was standing in front of a guard until the latter exercised his right to address you with an insult, as casually as a foreigner might say "hello." Their command of profanities was so impressive that I was surprised if a guard failed to open his mouth with a curse.

THE EVENING ASSEMBLY

What I am about to describe is the guards' most ingenious invention. In describing our daily routine, I have already mentioned a few of the innovations pioneered by these former students, although there were a few workers and janitors among them. Not all of them may have been academically gifted students, but as their former teacher, I must give them top marks for their management of the camp. Unfortunately, the curriculum at the university was largely theoretical, and as a professor, I must take some responsibility for this. But the students among our guards demonstrated all kinds of practical skills: They organized, managed, debated, lectured, accused, and made good on every threat to beat up a blackguard. In many ways, we were no match for them.

Their greatest invention, however, was the evening assembly, which consisted of the following ritual: After dinner, all the inmates would assemble in the small yard between two rows of blocks. A new speaker gave a lecture, usually a New Beida leader rather than one of the guards. The subject matter varied, since the aim was not strictly to expound on revolutionary principles, of which there weren't that many anyway—the speakers would soon have found themselves going over old material. Instead, the assembly was an exercise in the science of torment. The speakers spent each assembly seizing, so to speak, on inmates' pigtails: Each of us had various faults or "pigtails," and if you had none, they could easily be planted on you. There were two kinds of pigtails: minor incidents that had happened during the day's labor, and political errors in the written thought reports we submitted each day. All of us were extremely careful when working, not because we had learned the value of labor but because we were terrified of getting a beating—not that there was really any way to avoid one. If the guards had it in for you, they could always pick on your thought report. No matter how carefully you chose your words, the guards would have no trouble finding fault with one thing or another. After all, China has always been an empire of the written word, in which the dangers of verbal expression have a long history. The Qing dynasty emperor Yongzheng once had a general executed because he reversed the phrase *"zhao qian xi ti"* ("be diligent in the morning and alert at night"), altering the word order to write *"xi ti zhao qian"* instead.[2] Both expressions are equally laudatory, but the emperor's wrath had been aroused, so the man was beheaded. Our guards surpassed even the emperors of yore in combing our written reports for excuses to torment us. They always managed to find something, and the unlucky inmate they chose would be persecuted during the evening assembly.

The inmates would form four rows, which was as many as the yard could hold, and the evening always began with a roll call. One detail of the roll call made a lasting impression on me. An elderly professor of Western languages who had returned to China from overseas had been sentenced on some pretext to be "reformed." Confined to his bed and dying, he lived in a room next to the yard where inmates assembled. When his name was called, he always called out "Present!" from his wooden bed. His wavering voice brought tears to my eyes.

The rest of us stood there with our hearts thumping. Sometimes the guards laid hands on a man just as the speaker was barking his name out, before he had a chance to report to the front of the room. Using a common tactic of struggle sessions, they would twist his arms behind his back and grip his shoulders, kicking and punching him as they marched him out of the line. They might even force the inmate to the floor and kick him viciously or stamp on him. The sound of people being slapped in the face echoed in the nighttime air.

The assembly was a sight peculiar to the Cultural Revolution. We Chinese love our superlatives. We delight in disputing claims to being the best or biggest, but there was no room for argument in the assembly: It was easily Peking University's most popular attraction, drawing crowds on the scale of the changing of the guard at Buckingham Palace. As I stood there silently each day, hoping fervently that my name would not be called, I could just make out the faint shadows of onlookers crowding against the fence in the undergrowth. Under the dim electric lights, it was impossible to tell how many had come to admire the spectacle, but the crowd must have been at least several rows deep. Unfortunately for the city's tourism industry, unlike the centuries-old changing of the guard, the evening assemblies at Peking University only lasted for several months.

It is also a pity that our inquisitive friends didn't have the patience to linger until midnight, when they would have seen a far more sinister sight, one to which even inmates were not usually privy. One night, as I made my way toward the outhouse, I noticed several shadows under the trees in the yard, standing straight with both arms lifted as though they were embracing something. In fact, they were embracing thin air, and who knows how long the shadows had been standing there. I showed no emotion. But I reflected that this new stress position must be like holding the airplane position, and that I myself wouldn't last five minutes in it. I didn't know how much longer my fellow inmates would be forced to stand in that way, and as all inmates knew, it would be unwise to say that I had seen anything or make even the slightest sound. I slunk back to my room, and dreamed of men hugging emptiness.

EXTRAORDINARY RULES

In the blackguard camp, more and more unwritten rules ran parallel to the "Rules for Reform-Through-Labor Convicts." For instance, we were forbidden from looking up while walking, as well as from crossing our legs.

I may be no legal expert, but I've never read of a similar statute in any of the countries in which I've lived. Unless they are hunchbacked, people generally look where they are going as they walk—unless they are inmates of Peking University's cowshed. Did the guards come up with this rule on their own, or did they lift it from a torture manual one of them had inherited? Either way, it was the law, so we obeyed it. At all times and in all places, apart from one's own cell, looking up was strictly forbidden, especially when speaking to camp guards. Anyone who dared to look up would be slapped in the face or beaten. I always made sure that my gaze rested on the floor, or on a guard's shoes, since to lift one's eyes any higher would be too risky. I have distinct memories of the shoes the guards wore but only the blurriest impressions of the faces associated with those shoes. We were naturally permitted to hold our heads up when working, since if you are carrying a basket of coal, you have to look where you are going. Once, I looked up for a fraction of a second as we were lining up to go to lunch, and a guard roared, "Ji Xianlin, don't try anything funny!" I braced myself for a blow that never came. Never again would I try anything "funny."

Most people are in the habit of sometimes sitting with their legs crossed, but this too was forbidden in the cowshed. I remember reading somewhere that the military dictator Yuan Shikai always sat up straight, with his feet placed firmly next to each other on the ground.[3] But he was a soldier, whereas we inmates were all civilians—how could we be expected to match his military discipline?

I have already mentioned that the inmates had long since lost the ability to laugh. How can a basic human instinct be "lost," you ask? No, laughter wasn't forcibly stolen from us; we gave it up of our own accord. Under the constant threat of a beating, who was in the mood for laughter? Any laughter heard within the confines of the cowshed came from a guard. It sounded to me like the shrieking of owls at night and made me shiver with dread.

# IN THE COWSHED (2)

## THE INFORMANTS

THE GUARDS CONSOLIDATED their grip on power by operating a system of prison spies. I wondered whether they had copied this idea from the Gestapo, KGB, or the Kuomintang secret police, or if they had come up with it on their own. The spies were known as "informants," and the guards chose one per cell. The rest of us had no clue how they had been chosen or what they were instructed to do. Informants had various privileges, one of which was being allowed to return home every Sunday and to visit for longer durations. In the cowshed, some prisoners were never allowed to go home, while others were allowed home occasionally, rarely once a week. These privileges were naturally meted out by the guards, so informants snitched constantly, reporting even the smallest infractions in order to maintain their position. Some of them went out of their way to curry favor by taking note of which prisoners had been getting on the guards' nerves and informing on them. One day, I saw an informant lean over to whisper to a guard. As a result, a blackguard from his building was immediately dragged off to a room reserved for administering beatings. I didn't see what happened next, but it was all too easy to imagine the consequences.

EXTERNAL INVESTIGATORS

The interrogation of prisoners conducted by a work unit from outside Beijing was known as an external investigation. Many departments spared no expense in sending their representatives to remote villages in order to collect evidence against problematic individuals from their own department, so as to prevent them from ever being rehabilitated.

Since I had had the nerve to oppose Nie, her supporters held a particularly deep grudge against me and spent a lot of energy investigating my so-called crimes. When I was finally able to visit my hometown, a childhood friend from my village told me that he had met two investigators from Peking University who wanted to accuse me of being a landowner, and that he had told them off, declaring: "If anyone has a right to speak of hardship, it is Ji Xianlin!" They backed off, tails between their legs. But it seemed they returned to the village on another occasion to try their luck again. As I mentioned before, the Red Guards had confiscated my address book in the raid on my house so that they could "investigate" all the addresses in it. Other departments and work units were doing the same thing, so the country was crawling with external investigators.

The investigators I dealt with during my time in the cowshed each possessed a different style. Some of them gave me the names of the individuals under investigation, in which case I would simply be expected to write a report and hand it in to the guards. Some never raised their voice, whereas others were boorish and abusive. I was once summoned to the interrogation room to be interviewed by two investigators from Shandong University in my home province. I realized that a certain friend of mine must be under investigation. If I weren't a blackguard myself, I might have tried to help him, but by then I was powerless even to help myself. They pulled my hair, kicked and slapped me, treating me as though I was their own prisoner rather than an inmate of Peking University's cowshed. I watched them slam their fists on the table with rage. Their oily Shandong country accents and vulgar facial expressions disgusted me. The profanities of choice in Shandong differ from those in Beijing, but their import was all too clear. For two hours, the visitors did their best to bully me into confessing my own alleged crimes as well as my relationship with my friend. Even as a veteran of struggle sessions, I was stunned by their brazen insistence. I was drenched in sweat; it was well past lunchtime, and the interrogators had no intention of stopping. Finally the guards thought their guests were going too far and asked them to leave. I was exhausted, but I couldn't help thinking of my friend, who must have been having a rough time if he was up against these men.

ENDLESS STRUGGLE SESSIONS

As inmates of the cowshed, each day we would wait for guards or workers requesting labor to take us to a work site, like oxen being distributed to villagers by the head of the village commune's production team. We allowed ourselves to be led away like cattle; unlike oxen, we could speak, but we didn't make a sound.

*Laogai*, however, wasn't the only way in which we were to be reformed. Years of experience have taught me that labor only reforms the body; it cannot reform the soul. Labor can lacerate the convict's flesh with blisters and scars, but it cannot extinguish his anger. Labor must, as a result, be supplemented by the cruelty of struggle sessions. Those had predated the *laogai* camps, and the two were now being implemented in tandem.

Most prisoners probably preferred hard labor to struggle sessions, but since we had no choice in the matter, we simply had to be mentally prepared for either. Even if you had already been assigned to a work team, you could never feel perfectly safe. Prisoners were summoned to struggle sessions every day, and a department might suddenly decide to struggle against you, if only for entertainment. New Beida's Red Guards could stride into the cowshed office at any time, proudly wearing their armbands, and obtain permission from the overseers to struggle against you. I don't know exactly how many prisoners were sent to struggle sessions every day, but each one returned looking downcast, hair tangled, face covered with bruises.

As a former member of Jinggangshan, I was an especially frequent target of struggle sessions. Every morning at breakfast, I dreaded being told to stay behind from the day's work. When that happened, I would have to wait nervously in my room, dreading the struggle that awaited me, while my friends toiled blithely somewhere. The Red Guards would escort me into the yard, where I would be summoned to a sliding panel that faced the cowshed. The panel was covered with words, but I don't remember what they were. I would bow at the waist and wait for the guards to admonish me: "Ji Xianlin! Be good while you're being struggled against!" As if they were parents talking to a young child: "Be good while I'm away!" No matter where they took place, struggle sessions always proceeded along the same lines. They would begin with deafening slogans, followed by speeches and a bit of punching and slapping if the crowd became animated. Finally a voice would cut through the shouting and slogan-chanting: "Take Ji Xianlin away!" The ceremony finished, I would return home to the cowshed, as dejected as the others, my hair tangled like hay.

THE GREAT STRUGGLE SESSION OF JUNE 18, 1968

As mentioned earlier, June 18, 1966, was designated a day for struggling against "devils." I lay at home that day, as well as on June 18th the following year, since I had not yet been designated a devil. But by June 18, 1968, I was already a devil, and I had spent more than a month in the cowshed. I was finally eligible to participate. The guards seemed busy that morning, and it soon became clear that only a few inmates would have the honor of joining the procession. N. and I were the only two from our department. I have never forgotten the man who escorted us, Mr. Zhang, a worker in charge of educational technology. Not only did he refrain from insulting us, he was actually kind and polite. We inmates had stopped thinking of ourselves as ordinary people, and being treated humanely was a real shock.

But the rest of the audience wouldn't be so cordial. I didn't know who they were or where we were going, because I didn't dare look up. But as we left the cowshed, I realized we were walking past the lake and the Russian Building, up the slope past what is now the library, in the direction of the Philosophy Building. Eventually, after having been struggled against, we were taken back to the cowshed again. I don't remember listening to long speeches or being forced to hold the airplane position. The entire affair was chaotic, with hordes of people and intermittent shouts of "Down with..." probably organized by the many departments in attendance. Like a wandering spirit in a dream, I just kept my head down, dimly aware of the crowds around me even though I could only see their shoes and trousers. On the way back to the cowshed the crowds seemed to grow even bigger, and more bricks rained down on me. I was already completely numb to their blows. Only when I got back to the cowshed did I realize that someone had drawn a huge turtle on my shirt and tied a willow branch to it, perhaps to make a dog's tail. The cowshed suddenly seemed quiet, peaceful, almost like home.

I later reflected that the procession had only drawn such crowds because the masses had grown used to ordinary struggle sessions and no longer derived much pleasure from them. The annual struggle procession was thus a particularly festive occasion.

LIFE IN THE COWSHED

I have chosen a few anecdotes intended to offer a representative view of life in the cowshed. These anecdotes involve fellow blackguards of mine who will remain anonymous in my retelling, although anyone who was there at the time will recognize them: There will be no need for a *Concordance to the Cowshed.*

———

The professor of library science was an old friend of mine. He was a renowned scholar of the Dunhuang manuscripts and the former librarian of the Beijing Library.[1] Although I didn't know what he was accused of, I could've guessed that a man with his gifts wouldn't escape the cowshed. When we saw each other in the prison, neither of us said a word, as though we had both been struck dumb. But dumb though I may have been, I wasn't blind. I saw what happened to him.

One evening, to my surprise, this elderly professor was singled out during the evening assembly. The clear sound of a slap to the face was followed by more blows and savage kicking, until he was reduced to kneeling on the floor. It turned out that he had written his daily thought report on coarse toilet paper and dared to hand it to a guard in that form. This was one of the few instances that made me smile during our time in the cowshed. Had he used the coarse paper simply because there was no other paper available, or was he deliberately mocking the guards' self-importance? If the latter, his act of defiance is worth recording. I feared for him, but I also admired his nerve. To the rest of us prisoners, he was a hero.

———

The law school professor was an old Party cadre. All I know about him is that he joined the Party before the war. We met when he was first assigned to Peking University and asked me to translate the Manu-smṛti, one of the earliest texts of the Hindu Dharmaśāstra tradition. We continued to see each other at meetings on and off campus. He was down-to-earth and approachable, just as a cadre should be, and we got along very well. Of course, neither of us could have foreseen that we would eventually become fellow prisoners.

In the cowshed, blackguards avoided speaking to each other unless it was absolutely necessary. If you saw an acquaintance in the yard, you lowered your head and walked quickly by, without so much as lifting your eyes. We too never once acknowledged each other.

One Sunday, after the prisoners who had received permission to go home for the afternoon were returning to the cowshed, I saw this elderly professor holding a placard with his name on it and being forced by a guard to make the rounds of each cell. When he entered the cell, he said, "My name is ——, and I was late. I have been ordered to self-criticize. I admit I was wrong!" I don't know what the other prisoners thought, but I stood there, utterly embarrassed by his humiliation.

———

The lecturer in Mongolian studies was an unusually decent, honest person. During the Cultural Revolution, she was falsely accused of being a member of the Kuomintang's Three People's Principles Youth Corps, an assertion supported by neither evidence nor eyewitnesses. Her only crime, if she had one, was that of irreverence toward the power-hungry leader of New Beida. Some time earlier, N. and I had been assigned to clear the grounds outside the east gate of pebbles and loose bricks. One day this woman turned up to join us. Bewildered, I asked her whether the department's revolutionary committee had sent her. They hadn't, she said.

"So what are you doing here?"

"They told me I'm guilty, so I started feeling guilty and decided to reform myself through labor."

I was puzzled by her explanation, which seemed to be motivated by something like the Christian notion of original sin. That was the sort of person she was. But given that I was a blackguard myself and under orders "not to speak out of turn," I didn't dare say anything else to her.

Unsurprisingly, she wasn't among the convicts who were transported to Taiping Village some time later. But trouble wasn't far off. One day at dusk, a new prisoner was dragged into the cowshed. I glanced over surreptitiously and recognized her. I had thought she had escaped the cowshed, but here she was, and this time it didn't look like she had volunteered. I pretended to look the other way. "What is your name?" a guard asked her.

She gave her full name, which ended with the character *hua*.

"Which *hua*?"

"The *hua* in Zhonghua Minguo," she said, using the taboo term for Taiwan, "Republic of China."

How dare this "active counterrevolutionary" invoke the Republic of China in a cowshed representing the full authority of the revolutionary committee? She was immediately punched and kicked to the ground. Then one guard had an idea: He took her to a tree with a crooked, low-hanging branch, and forced her to stand beneath the branch so that her head was just touching it.

"One step forward!" said the guard.

To take a step forward, she had to tilt her head back.

"Another step!"

The branch sloped down, forcing her to tip her body as well as her head backward.

"Another step!"

Here the branch became very low. She was no circus performer, so this was as far as she could fit. The commands ceased, and she stood there, bent over backward at the waist. Unable to hold this position for even a minute, she collapsed on the ground, drenched in sweat. Needless to say, this didn't end well for her. She had just become the unlucky victim of the guards' newest method for torturing people. The next day her face was swollen with bruises.

———

Having spent decades serving in an administrative capacity at Peking University, I had known the Party branch secretary of the Biology Department for years. He was immediately singled out as a capitalist-roader at the beginning of the revolution, and had been a target of the first June 18th struggle session, so he had ample experience of class struggle.

For some reason, the Biology Department was full of the Empress Dowager's supporters, and there were many biology students among the guards. By the time the cowshed was built, attention had shifted away from the capitalist-roaders who had been targeted in earlier struggle sessions. Very few of them were imprisoned along with us, the counterrevolutionary academic authorities, so I was surprised to see this man in the cowshed.

The many biology students among the guards took particular pleasure in tormenting him; while I don't know all the details of what he suffered, I myself witnessed one chilling instance of his treatment.

On a July or August day when the sun was at its hottest, I caught sight of the Party secretary staring at the noonday sun. A guard, a biology student, was sitting nearby in the shade.

At the time I was puzzled by the sight, but later I heard that the guard had devised the following punishment: Open your eyes wide, look straight at the sun, and don't blink or you'll get a beating. I shuddered. From ancient feudal societies built on slavery to modern capitalist societies, has anyone devised a punishment like this? Was it even humanly possible to look at the sun for longer than a split second without going blind?

Two other blackguards from that department offended another guard who was a biology student. He ordered them to stand back to back a few steps apart in the courtyard, and lean backward so that their heads touched—the only way they could avoid falling over was to push their heads against each other. Other such incidents that I won't list here prove that our tormentors made rapid progress in the arts of torture.

---

She was a teacher in the elementary school attached to the university. I didn't know her personally and don't know why she was imprisoned in the cowshed.

Over the course of several months, I noticed there was a distinct allocation of labor among the guards when it came to torturing us. This woman, for instance, was always beaten by the same guard. One morning I noticed that her arm was bandaged and in a sling. People were saying that her tormentor had broken her arm during a vicious beating in the interrogation room. She had to come to work anyway. Inquiring into anything was fatal for a blackguard, so I did my best to forget what I had seen, and that was all I ever learned about the episode.

---

Before the cowshed, I had never met or heard of Zhou, an older student in the Western Languages Department.

Since the first campaigns of the Anti-Rightist Movement in 1957, as an "old rightist" Zhou must have survived a decade of being persecuted in political campaigns. By the time I met him, his face was as yellow as wax and swollen, most of his hair was gone, and he looked like an elderly, sick man. He was said to have been an intelligent and promising student, but years of physical and mental torture had reduced him to little more than an idiot. Despite living in constant fear for my own life, terrified of the guards' spears, I felt sorry for him.

The Red Guards callously treated the idiot as a two-legged plaything and loved to ridicule and humiliate him. He was assigned to a clever-looking young worker who could beat him up whenever he felt like it. Even on the way to the cafeteria, the worker was constantly abusing the idiot. At night we often heard his cries from the interrogation room. In this memoir I have generally tried to avoid calling people names, but I am going to break my own rule here: That worker was a thug, worse than a pig or dog.

One day, someone painted a large turtle in white on the back of the idiot's shirt. He wandered about, looking lost. His clothes were filthy, since they had probably not been washed since he came to the cowshed; against the shirt, the turtle looked dazzling white and could be seen even from a distance. Other people might've found the sight hilarious, but we prisoners, having lost the privilege of laughter, kept our pity and revulsion to ourselves.

———

The physics lecturer was the only son of an elderly professor in the Psychology Department, and one of his legs was visibly shorter than the other. I had not met him before. One day, not long after lunch, I heard the unmistakable sound of someone being thrashed either with a cudgel or a bicycle chain wrapped in rubber. (There was no break after lunch for us in the cowshed. N. was once found dozing in his chair after lunch and tortured for an hour outside, possibly also forced to stare at the sun.) I was already numb to this sound, which could be heard several times a day. But the beating lasted longer and sounded more brutal than usual, so I glanced out the window and saw the disabled man lying at the entrance of the cowshed, while the guards continued to flog him. I couldn't see if they were kicking him, but he was lying on the ground, his face caked with blood.

The physics lecturer joined the cowshed relatively late, and I wondered how he ended up with us. Like Hu Shi, I have an interest in historical accuracy, but I don't have the heart to seek it. From that point on, whenever we lined up to have dinner in the cafeteria, we were joined by the new inmate with an asymmetrical gait.

———

I have many other memories, but I cannot bear to go on. The reader may be able to form a clear impression of life in the cowshed from these incidents.

# IN THE COWSHED (3)

## THE VIP ROOM

I KNEW THE Buddhist hell had eighteen levels, but it took a while before I discovered that hell in the cowshed might have deeper recesses than the one I lived in. To explain how I came to this realization, I must begin by introducing Zhang Guoxiang, a biology student who wasn't one of the original guards of the cowshed but had been sent there later by Nie's revolutionary committee. If I ever wondered why, I knew better than to ask. Zhang stood out not because he was particularly high-ranking but because he was always poking his nose into everything. The guards could take whatever they wanted from inmates' homes; just as our lives were at their mercy, our property was now theirs. Zhang confiscated a bicycle from a convict's home and often rode it around the yard for fun. No one else did anything for fun in the silent terror that blanketed the cowshed, so this, too, attracted attention.

After the evening assembly, or sometimes even after the regulation bedtime of ten o'clock, Zhang could be found sitting beneath the brightly lit tree in the center of the yard with his right leg planted on a chair. He'd be picking at the dirt beneath his toenails and railing at the unlucky convict who stood before him with bowed head. There was nothing special about his rants, but his unusual posture made an impression on me. One night I was surprised to find Lu Ping standing before Zhang. A principal target of the Empress Dowager's big-character posters, Lu Ping had previously been imprisoned elsewhere and was only moved to the cowshed later on. I didn't know what he asked Lu, how long the interrogation lasted, or what came of it. But something about the whole scene looked suspicious to me.

Little did I know that I would be standing in Lu Ping's position only a few nights later. Not long after the curfew bell rang, I heard someone call my name from the direction of the Democracy Building. Even at night, I was always extremely alert, and I rushed to the front yard right away. There I found Zhang sitting with his leg perched as usual on his chair, cupping his ankle in his right hand.

"Why have you been corresponding with foreign spy agencies?"

"I have not."

"Why did you say that Comrade Jiang Qing has been giving New Beida morphine shots?"

"That was just a metaphor."

"How many wives do you have?"

I was taken by surprise. "I don't have several wives," I replied carefully.

We had a few more exchanges of this sort before he said, "I have been very kind to you tonight." He was right. I hadn't been beaten up or even yelled at, and I ought to be as relieved as though I were the subject of an imperial amnesty. But the word "tonight" should have aroused my suspicions.

The following night, after the curfew bell had rung and I was getting ready for bed, I heard a voice yell: "Ji Xianlin!" I rushed toward the yard even faster than yesterday, and ran into Zhang just around the corner of the building. He was fuming: "Where have you been? Are you deaf?"

Before I knew what was happening, a series of blows rained down on my head. I could tell that Zhang's weapon of choice was a bicycle chain wrapped in rubber. There was a ringing sound in my ears, and I seemed to see stars, but I stood there rigidly without flinching, not daring to move. My eyes, mouth, and nose were burning with pain. I willed myself not to faint. I was so disoriented that I could barely hear Zhang screaming at me. The convicts who lived on that block later told me that the beating had lasted longer than usual, and they spoke of the incident with fear in their eyes. I was barely conscious when I finally heard the command: "Get lost!" Realizing that the wrathful god was being merciful to me again, I hurried back to my room with my tail between my legs.

As soon as I recovered slightly, I became acutely aware of the pain. I examined myself: My nose and ears were bleeding, but none of my teeth had been knocked out, and I could still open my swollen eyes. I writhed in bed all night long, my whole body aching, my open wounds sticky with blood. Without a mirror, I could only guess what I must look like. When Zhang's victims appeared the following morning, their faces were always swollen with bruises, and I figured I must be in an even worse state. The following day, I went through the usual routine of working and learning Mao's sayings, but my mind was blank. I didn't even think about suicide.

Zhang wasn't through with me yet. He barged into my hut at noon and ordered me to move to a different cell. It wasn't as though I had to pack: I simply rolled up my bedding and brought it to a room that faced the place where I had been beaten. By day it seemed no different from my previous cell, but at night I realized that this was the VIP (Very Important Prisoners) room. The lights stayed on all night, and none of the prisoners slept as we each took turns keeping watch. Were the guards afraid we would try to escape? Surely this couldn't be the case since intellectuals are the most timid of prisoners. This may have been a measure to prevent suicides, in case anyone wanted to hang themselves, for example. I realized that after my beating I had earned a promotion to a deeper level of hell, analogous to death row or to the Avici circle of the Buddhist hell. Lu Ping also lived here.

Zhang forced me and Professor Wang to fetch water for the entire camp. Three times a day, we hauled a cartful of drinking water from the public water tank back to the cowshed. I don't know how Professor Wang managed to end up in the same boat as me—he had committed no crimes and had never been a member of Jinggangshan. Fetching water was backbreaking work, and we did it together three times a day on top of our usual work and memorization. We looked on hungrily as the other inmates ate. Whenever it rained, we got soaked. But Professor Wang always found a way to enjoy himself. When we reached the tank he would secretly make himself a cup of tea and light up a cigarette.

THE SPECIAL GROUP

The guards were politically astute types. Having assembled all the cow devils and reformed us for more than half a year with memorization, lectures, and physical punishment, they decided it was time to cause divisions among us. They did so by selecting a group of convicts and designating them the Special Group.

The Special Group was housed in the Foreign Languages Building. Neither of the doors to the building could be opened, so a window was used as the entrance, and a long wooden plank served as a path into the classroom. I had no idea what the classroom was like, but I envied the convicts in this group enormously. I could endure beatings, hunger, and thirst for the time being, but it was the absence of hope that things would ever change which drove me to despondency. The future seemed to be an endless sea with no boat to board, no island in sight. Now that the Special Group was organized, it seemed like the boat that would carry me over the seas. Being selected for the group became my only ambition.

Members of the group had several enviable privileges. They were permitted to wear Chairman Mao lapel pins, and they could leave work early or arrive late. They may even have been allowed the privilege of paying Party membership fees. Whenever I overheard them singing songs in praise of the Great Leader, I imagined what it would be like to step onto that long wooden plank and find myself inside the classroom. It was unclear whether the Special Group was subject to a different set of rules, or whether the rules were just less strictly enforced. For instance, they actually crossed their legs in the cowshed, whereas I wouldn't dare. They seemed to hold their heads a little higher when walking. But for some reason, no member of the Special Group was ever released until the cowshed was dismantled.


AN INDONESIAN LANGUAGE INSTRUCTOR IN THE EASTERN
LANGUAGES DEPARTMENT

This individual had been a student in the Eastern Languages Department in Nanking University before Liberation, and when he transferred to Peking University he stayed on to teach after graduating. He was talented, hardworking, and produced excellent academic work. When he was studying in Indonesia, his family had run into financial difficulties, and I had done what I could to help him. We were on very good terms, and he always treated me with great respect.

But when Peking University split into rival factions, he joined New Beida. Overnight, he became extremely hostile toward me. He came to every struggle session that targeted me, and he glared with more ferocity and slammed his fists on the table with more vigor than anyone else, going out of his way to prove his allegiance to the Empress Dowager. Perhaps he was terrified that someone would discover he used to oppose the Communist Party and the Soviet Union. Although I had been warned about fair-weather friends, I found his betrayal particularly difficult to accept.

Class struggle eventually caught up with him. One morning I walked out of the cowshed and was about to bow my head as required, when I saw a big-character poster on the sidewalk: "Down with ——, the counterrevolutionary!"

I was stunned. Not too long ago he had been aggressive and brimming with revolutionary zeal as part of a panel that interrogated me. It turned out that someone had finally discovered the skeletons in his closet. That night, he took a capitalist overdose of sleeping pills and "alienated himself from the people."

I took no pleasure in the news. Life is too complicated and terrible for gloating.

## GIVING UP ON MYSELF

After a few months in the cowshed, I could feel my emotions growing duller and my thoughts more stupid by the day. The cowshed may not have been hell, but it felt as close to it as I could imagine; I may not have been a hungry ghost, but I certainly was as hungry as one. I felt like neither man nor devil, or perhaps like both man and devil. I began to judge myself the way I knew other people judged me. I used to consider myself a human being, and treated myself as one. But to borrow a popular philosophical term, I now felt alienated from myself.

Without wanting to sound arrogant, I should say up front that if there are two kinds of people, good guys and bad guys, as children say, I profess to be one of the good guys. I've never been particularly avaricious or stingy. When I was a young teenager, the pharmacist's clerk in Jinan once gave me one silver coin too many in change. A silver coin was a small fortune to a child like me, but I gave it back to him right away. The clerk blushed, and I later realized that he might have been embarrassed because he wouldn't have been so honest himself. In 1946, when I was about to return to China from Europe, while in Switzerland I sold a gold watch in order to send some money home, and exchanged the remaining francs for gold. The man made a mistake and gave me an extra ounce of gold; again, a single ounce was worth a significant sum of money, but I returned it right away. These are only small examples, but they mean something to an ordinary person like me.

In the cowshed, on the other hand, I gradually grew accustomed to the idea that I had become a cow devil, although I had initially resisted the transformation. I stopped distinguishing between man and devil, beauty and ugliness, right and wrong. As the proverb goes, a cracked jug may as well be smashed, and I had given up on myself as though I were a cracked jug. I was no longer tempted by suicide, nor did I think about the future. I had simply stopped caring who I was or what people thought of me.

I also had other, more pressing worries. The living allowance allotted to my family was pitiful, and even if we ate nothing but corn-meal buns with pickled vegetables, we would starve. A meager diet devoid of any meat meant that the hard labor made me constantly hungry. Sometimes I trailed the guards around, begging them for empty cartons of tofu, so that I could dip my cornmeal buns into the thin liquid at the bottom of the cartons. On one occasion, I was made to clean out Blocks 28 and 29, student dormitories that had been damaged during fighting by the rival factions. In a large room littered with debris on the south side of Block 28, I found a couple of moldy steamed buns in a bamboo cooker. Without stopping to think about hygiene or germs, I pocketed my finds and wolfed them down furtively when the guards weren't looking.

I learned to tell lies. When I was at a work site and unbearably hungry, I would tell the team leader that I had to go to the hospital.

With permission to leave, I would scurry home by back alleys no one used, gulp down a couple of steamed buns with sesame paste, and hurry back to work as though I had just been to the doctor. Of course, I risked grim consequences if I ran into a guard or one of their informants.

I was once thrilled to find some ten-cent and twenty-cent notes on the road, and quickly stuffed them into my pocket. A convict was prohibited from holding his head up when walking; from then on, I turned the rule to my advantage and kept my eyes peeled for copper coins. When I realized the latrines in the cowshed were the best place to find coins, the outhouse shunned by everyone else became one of my favorite spots.

I wouldn't have believed I could do such unimaginably base things until I actually did them. I lost all sense of shame, as well as my sense of right and wrong. Just recalling those times makes me shudder. I used to wonder how one could morally corrupt a person, and I assumed that some people are just innately depraved. Now I know from personal experience that the truth is far more complex, but that no one can be held responsible for another's evil.

———

There are many other things that can be said about life in the cowshed, but I will stop here. I trust that none of my readers will now doubt the validity of the Law of Maximum Torment. It is unclear what the Red Guards achieved from torturing us: They never discussed their motivations, and there is no way to guess. Their official aim was to effect "reform through labor," but although labor may have disciplined our bodies, it couldn't reform our souls. As my own experience shows, persecution doesn't purify its victims—it only corrupts them. That is all I have to say regarding the Law of Maximum Torment.

# RELOCATING THE COWSHED

WITH THE ARRIVAL of winter, stoves were installed in the huts. Even though we were only allocated enough coal to light a few small fires, our cell felt snug in comparison to the bitter cold outside.

The number of inmates dwindled, and when there were only a few of us left, we were all moved into one large building. I didn't dare ask why. Now that I was already in the Avici circle of hell, I decided that things could hardly get much worse.

There were so few of us that the building seemed empty. The rats grew bold and scuttled about in broad daylight. I found them gnawing on a dried steamed bun I had brought from home, and when I tried to chase them away, they glared at me with their little eyes and hid on the windowsill. Perhaps even the rats had realized that the building was inhabited not by ordinary human beings but by blackguards whom they could bully if they felt like it.

"Every wall has its cracks," as the saying goes. Although the blackguards lacked the courage to speak freely or send each other messages, I gradually discovered that Nie's revolutionary committee had altered its policy of housing all *laogai* convicts together, and that each department was to take responsibility for its own blackguards. Eventually, my department claimed its own, and we were relocated to the Foreign Languages Building.

Not long ago, when the Special Group was housed there, I had set my heart on being moved to the Foreign Languages Building too. But now that I was moved in, I was still an ordinary blackguard, my status unchanged. We blackguards were assigned to the Burmese language classroom on the north side of the second floor where we slept on mats on the floor. Our guard slept on a large table near the window, surveying us from above. He was a young student called Lu, nicknamed Lujiang, or "Tinker." To my surprise, there were new arrivals among us, and I wondered whether they were *laogai* convicts too. Because we were all in the same boat, we got along well.

Life became less dramatic. I was no longer constantly on edge as I had been in the cowshed. Since Tinker slept in our room, I stopped straining to make sure I wouldn't miss hearing a guard's orders and get in trouble.

But I couldn't forget that I was still a blackguard. Many of the offices on this floor belonged to the department that I had headed for twenty years before being struggled against, and I knew the rooms inside out. This used to be my turf, and I had felt at home here. Now times had changed, and I was a blackguard rather than a professor. The tenth-century poet Li Yu wrote: "Spring passes, as a flower falls to the ground or water flows in a stream, and the past seems as distant as the heavens are from the earth." The past seemed distant to me now that I had spent more than a year labeled as a counterrevolutionary. I felt no desire to regain my former position. I had already been struggled against and excluded, and my only aim was to survive.

There were three places in the building I was allowed to enter: my cell, the toilet, and the interrogation room, the location of which shifted constantly. The second was shared by both counterrevolutionaries and revolutionaries, since the cow devils weren't really devils and we needed to relieve ourselves as well. It remains to be seen whether real devils share this need.

For the blackguards to be living in close quarters with ordinary civilians was a little uncomfortable—we often ran into each other. The Chinese are a courteous people, and failing to greet someone you know is unthinkable. There are fewer variations of greetings in Chinese than in English with "hello," "good morning," "how do you do," and so on. (The Chinese sometimes say "good morning," but that is a recently imported phrase.) The universal greeting across China regardless of the time of day is, "Have you already eaten?" In the Foreign Languages Building, when I ran into someone I had known for years, I couldn't bring myself to use greetings of either the imported or nationally common variation. Instead, I would look down and slink away. I don't know how my acquaintances felt, but we blackguards constantly felt rather awkward. Sometimes in the corridors we could hear ordinary people talking and laughing in a room, their voices full of a proletariat gaiety inaccessible to us. Laozi wrote of small, bordering kingdoms where the people could hear the other kingdom's dogs barking, and yet each kingdom was completely self-sufficient. We, too, seemed to live in a kingdom separate from that of ordinary people. Despite being able to hear their voices, we ourselves were voiceless, like so many shadows.

No one was brave enough to pass me any news, and so I found out what was happening by eavesdropping on the chatter in the corridors. The first newsworthy incident concerned the lecturer in Mongolian studies mentioned earlier, the only female inmate from the department. In the Foreign Languages Building, there was no designated cell for women as there had been in the cowshed, and housing her with the men was out of the question, so she had to be put in a separate room. The female wardens in charge of her were a student of Korean and Ye, the department librarian. Ye was a minx, a troublemaker, a gossiping, brutal type. Our department used the library as a common room, and rumors always started there. During the Cultural Revolution, Ye joined New Beida and became a rabid supporter of the Empress Dowager. Once she even came to my home, snapping and snarling, to haul me off to a struggle session, even though it was almost unheard of for a female Red Guard to escort a male prisoner. So when she was put in charge of the only female convict in the department, she wasn't going to let her get off so easily. That night, she and a few others decided to interrogate the woman and beat her up severely. I found out that this had happened, but I had grown so used to incidents like this that I was totally numb.

Little did I know that the next newsworthy incident would involve me.

No one had lifted a finger against me since we moved to the Foreign Languages Building. I had not learned my lesson; I was still very stubborn, and despite having gone through the hell that was the cowshed, I refused to make false confessions. One day, Zhao Liangshan (it is said that he is no longer alive), an army major who had been sent to support the leftists at the university, summoned me to his office to question me. I was disappointed and thought that a soldier of the People's Liberation Army would be more reasonable. "All my diaries were confiscated and are being held somewhere in this building," I snapped. "It would only take you five minutes to check them and find out what I did that day." This angered him. His face darkened, and he told me off for being uncooperative. He was the boss here—how dare I answer back?

When we returned to our cell after dinner, a lecturer who used to oppose the Empress Dowager brought a team of people to the cell. They plastered the walls with political banners, giving our blank walls a dash of color. The slogans were entirely predictable. "Ji Xianlin has been uncooperative, down with Ji Xianlin!" "Resistance will be punished!" "No speaking out of line!" I was so used to being struggled against that I slept soundly anyway.

Sure enough, Red Guards from my department—probably representing both factions—came for me the following day. Unable to lift my head as I was marched away, I only gradually realized that they were taking me to the student dorm Block 40. I could make out posters with slogans, and though I couldn't read them, it wasn't hard to guess that they'd be full of insults and slander. I had become the poster child for uncooperative blackguards.

I was dragged by the scruff of my neck into the building, down the narrow corridors crammed full of students. Slogans rang in my ears and fists rained down on me. Unable to make out a single face, I walked (or, rather, was made to walk) from one end of the corridor to another on the first floor, and did the same on the second and third floors. Eventually, just as I was getting bored of the whole exercise, I was taken back to the Foreign Languages Building. I later heard that this was called an "indoor struggle procession." It may even have been invented by the students in my department—if so, it deserves to be recorded in any future *History of the Great Proletariat Cultural Revolution*. Given that I had already survived much worse, I was mostly just amused.

Major Zhao must have been up all night planning the next installment of struggle sessions. Immediately after breakfast, a student came to take me to another one. When I was allowed to look up, I realized I was in a staff room with its usual occupants and a few other students. I was preparing myself to hold the airplane position, so I was startled to be given a chair and permitted to sit down. What could come of a struggle session conducted with its victim sitting? Again, I grew bored and shut my ears to the commotion until I heard the order: "Take Ji Xianlin out!" The show was over.

As I was getting ready to go back to my cell, however, I was dragged to another staff room where the process started all over again. Then there was a third room and a fourth—I lost track of the number of struggle sessions, but there were more than a dozen staff rooms in the department, so I must have been struggled at least as many times. Next it was the students' turn. Each one of the twenty classes had to struggle me once, which should have added up to more than thirty hours altogether, though it probably didn't take quite that long since some classes skimped, and the quality of the struggle sessions was variable. For the next few days I was busier than an itinerant actor: We did eight or nine sessions a day, one after another, stopping only for meals. It was a little tiring, but I grew to enjoy this sort of struggle, in which I could let other people shout themselves hoarse while I sat quietly, letting my mind wander.

Remaining uncooperative from beginning to end saved me from committing suicide in the early days of the revolution, while toward the end it gave me a chance to enjoy a milder variant of struggle sessions. This certainly wasn't what the revolutionaries had anticipated.

# HALF LIBERATED

I WAS TO be half released or "liberated" from prison. As there was no official definition of what being half released meant, I will relate my experience here.

By the time the many struggle sessions had ended, the new year was upon us. Shortly before Chinese New Year in 1969, the department's revolutionary committee suddenly notified me that I was now permitted to return home. Tinker escorted me to my place, though now that I was no longer a prisoner he was technically not acting as a guard. The larger of our two rooms was locked, and my aunt and wife had been living in a tiny room of a hundred square feet. They told me that for some time, a student repeatedly returned with the confiscated key to our big room, bringing a woman with him. They would sleep on my bed and cook with our gas. They threatened my aunt and wife not to tell anyone. Now Tinker opened the door to my room with that same key. By then, I had not slept in my own bed for eight or nine months.

I was immensely relieved but also apprehensive. I was still labeled a counterrevolutionary, and the future seemed bleak. My meager allowance barely fed our family. Eventually it was increased, though I don't remember when this happened or how much more I received.

But I continued to be persecuted. Once I overheard the head of the Family and Dependents Committee in our building, an old man said to be a former Kuomintang soldier, announce loudly to the whole building: "Ji Xianlin is back! Watch him carefully." It seemed likely that he was acting under orders from his superiors. Even though I was used to that kind of rhetoric, I couldn't help feeling a little uneasy at having been sentenced to "surveillance by the people." I had become an untouchable, like an HIV carrier or plague victim.

Even if my neighbors hadn't reminded me that I was to be shunned, I would still have to adjust to acting normally around other people again. I still stared at the ground wherever I walked. In shops, I didn't dare greet the shop assistants as "comrade"—how dare I see myself as their comrade? But then what should I call them? Addressing them as "sir" or "miss" was inappropriate in the revolutionary era; not greeting them at all would be even worse. I found myself stuttering with embarrassment as though I was already losing my mind in old age.

Before long, I was ordered to begin studying in Block 40. It was about two miles from my home and the roads were icy; the walk would take half an hour even if I hurried. I decided not to take the main road and instead to cross the frozen lake. It suddenly occurred to me that I was both literally and metaphorically walking on thin ice. I had no idea what the future held or how to behave now that I had been released. When I saw the guard outside Block 40, should I still cringe and address him deferentially like a prisoner would? When I saw a Red Guard, should I cry "Reporting" and hang my head? Realizing that I had no answers for any of these questions, I began to linger and drag my feet.

When I finally reached Block 40, I couldn't help thinking of being paraded through these corridors just yesterday. Now that I was neither professor nor prisoner, what was my new identity? Apprehensively, I reported to the department headquarters and was relieved to be greeted with indifference. No one was going to beat me up or shout slogans at me. I was assigned to a group of students studying Hindi and began to help with their lessons and activities. I soon found that all the blackguards in my department were here, and that we had each been allocated different jobs. I was ordered to sweep the corridors with a few other lecturers, while a lecturer of Hindi who had been unjustly labeled a landowner was assigned to scrub the toilets. I had come prepared to be assigned the dirtiest jobs, and I was surprised when that didn't happen.

I wasn't used to mixing among the masses, and I felt uneasy about being neither man nor devil. The students were young and full of energy. During recess they would take out their musical instruments and sing or play music. I was moved by one student's playing on the *erhu*, but I couldn't allow myself to enjoy it too much.[1] I sat stiffly like a wooden statue in the thick of their laughter and chatter, acutely aware of not fitting in.

Things improved, but a few complications still loomed. To begin with, there was the question of my Party dues. As I have mentioned, prisoners in the cowshed didn't pay dues. Since I couldn't draw my own salary, my elderly aunt did so for me. Each month she would go to the Foreign Languages Building to collect the forty-odd yuan on which our family of three survived. People would whisper behind her back or even insult her because I was a blackguard and a Jinggang-shan man to boot. She simply put up with the humiliation. But even under these circumstances, she was still worried that her nephew might lose his Party membership, so she kept paying dues on my behalf. Surprisingly, she found a member of the department's revolutionary committee who was willing to accept my dues without reporting me, or I could've expected a beating. I don't know who that person was, but I remain grateful to him or her to this day. My aunt also said that one Comrade Yuan never insulted her and was always kind to her, telling her to take care of herself and make sure she kept her cash safe. His kindness was like a glimmer of warmth on a winter night, and she always spoke of him with gratitude.

Now that I had been transferred to Block 40, I ought to be responsible for paying my Party dues. But what with my own ambiguous status and the state of confusion within the Party itself, I barely even knew whom to give my dues to. After some time, a senior member of the department summoned me to ask why I hadn't paid my membership dues. "Once I am formally expelled from the Party, I will repay every cent I owe," I told him candidly, thinking there was no chance I would be allowed to retain my membership.

I was also troubled about returning to Block 40, a place I knew extremely well. By 1966, I had chaired the Eastern Languages Department for twenty years; the department's male students also lived in this block, so I had come here often. I had memories of being warmly welcomed to Block 40, as well as memories of being mercilessly humiliated. I don't want to make trite remarks about the fragility of interpersonal relationships—this has always been part of the human condition, the norm rather than the exception. But my own feelings were fragile. I was no hero and had no desire to become one; heroes are made of sterner stuff. I was an ordinary human being, with run-of-the-mill hopes and fears, trying to recover from my experience in the cowshed. Things had certainly improved since I had been transferred to Block 40, but my future was very much uncertain, and Block 40 was the locus of many memories.

To speak only of the few years following the start of the Cultural Revolution, much had taken place in Block 40. In 1966, after returning from Nankou, I was standing outside the compound when I saw the poster criticizing me and couldn't help sniffing audibly with disapproval. I was later told to hand over three thousand yuan and hurried to Block 40 to give it to the students, who then refused to accept the cash. When I watched the struggle sessions targeting capitalist-roaders at the very beginning of the revolution, it was Block 40 that shook with their slogans. When I offended an army captain, I was subjected to an indoor struggle procession here in Block 40.

And now I was in Block 40 again, living and working as one of the masses once more.

## IN YANQING XINHUA CAMP

This time around, I spent less than a year in Block 40, from the winter of 1969 through part of autumn the following year. During this period, the famed 8341 Special Regiment, the same regiment responsible for the personal security of Central Government leaders, sent troops to Peking University to help support the leftists. Because they were known to have a long-standing revolutionary tradition, many teachers and students, myself included, hoped they would put things right at Peking University. Yanyuan was still overrun by factional fighting, and we looked to the regiment to bring order to the campus.

Instead, most of the professors at the university were shipped off to Liyuzhou in Jiangxi to be reformed through labor under the leadership of the 8341 Special Regiment. Liyuzhou is known to be blistering hot and inundated with parasitic blood flukes. One of the army officers dubbed this new plan for tormenting the intellectuals the "heat treatment." I steeled myself for yet another ordeal and made preparations for the trip. Unexpectedly, I was sent with the students of Hindi and Thai to be reeducated by peasants at the Yanqing Xinhua Camp in the suburbs of Beijing.

I soon discovered that I had a special role to fulfill. It had apparently been decided that criticism meetings were incomplete without a live target to criticize, and I was the designated target. My role reminded me of the sheep tied on top of cars driving in the countryside of Xinjiang. When a good spot is found by the picnickers, they slaughter the sheep on the spot, cook a lamb pilaf, and return home satiated. At Xinhua Camp, I mostly worked in the vegetable cellar; I was criticized at one meeting. I knew that I was fulfilling my role.

By Chinese New Year of 1970, we were summoned back to Beijing.

# FULLY LIBERATED

THIS CHAPTER DESCRIBES "complete liberation" while the previous one describes "half liberation." These are general concepts rather than technically precise terms. A rigorous discussion of the difference between the two is best left to legal scholars or philosophers.

Being back on campus lifted my spirits. At around this time, the department moved its offices into Block 35; like nearly every other department, we were moving into the student dorms in order to be close to the students and facilitate the "student-led management and reform" of the university. According to this new policy, lecturers were to be managed by students, beginners were to devise the curriculum of more advanced students, and so on.

Block 35 was a four-story building. The women lived on the third and fourth floors, and the men lived on the first and second floors. A few rooms had been set aside on the second floor as the Party office for the department. I was assigned to the guardroom, a tiny cubicle on the first floor with a large window facing onto a walking path. As the security guard, my tasks were to guard the building, to man the telephone, and to distribute all correspondence. The job appeared straightforward, but it was easier said than done. In guarding the building, for instance, I knew all the lecturers and older students but none of the newer students, which meant I simply had to let everyone in. As for the telephone, I answered calls when they came in and sat idle otherwise. Most of the calls seemed to be for the women, which meant making multiple trips to the third and fourth floors to alert the recipient. Climbing stairs is said to be an excellent way of getting exercise, but after trying a few times, I decided that making dozens of trips a day was not for me. I gave up and decided to simply shout up toward the windows from the ground floor. This worked, even though it meant that some of the women in north-facing rooms couldn't hear me, which sometimes caused trouble. I ignored it, having decided that I was already doing the best I could. Finally, I brought all newspapers to the office and collected any letters that came in the post, leaving the mail on the windowsill to be picked up by the recipients.

These three tasks made the days pass quickly. Every day at eight I walked from Block 13 in the staff quarters to Block 35 in the dorms, and went home at noon. Then I returned to work at two in the afternoon, and got home at six. I was in excellent health, since I had few worries and got plenty of exercise from walking several miles a day. At some point, my original salary was reinstated. I had no teaching or research responsibilities, and no one dared write to me or come to see me. I was beginning to enjoy my life as an "untouchable."

## TRANSLATING THE *RAMAYANA*

I was used to writing all the time, and I gradually grew tired of my mindless existence. When no phone calls or letters came, I sat alone behind my big glass window watching people come in and out. This became very dull. "How can a lifetime be frittered away save by finding something unprofitable to do?" I thought of these ancient words of wisdom. Why shouldn't I find something to do? Some unprofitable pursuit—mahjong, for instance—was out of the question, and I couldn't bring myself to start writing. Finally I hit upon the idea of beginning a translation. Since it seemed as if I might spend the rest of my working life as the security guard of Block 35, I decided to translate the longest and most difficult text I could think of. It would certainly be unprofitable, if nothing else, since no publisher would dare to publish a translation by someone like me. I finally settled on the *Ramayana*, one of the two great Indian epics. It consists of some twenty thousand verses, mostly of four lines each. I figured it would keep me busy for several years.

I requested that the department librarian order an authoritative new edition of the *Ramayana* in Sanskrit from India via the International Bookstore, expecting nothing to come of it as it was extremely difficult to obtain foreign books at the time. But I was in luck: Within weeks, all eight volumes of the Sanskrit original were sitting on my desk. This was the best thing that had happened to me since the Cultural Revolution began. The sight of the books refreshed me and brought a long-forgotten smile to my face.

I didn't want to risk bringing the books with me to work. I was, after all, a security guard, and I was keenly aware of the shadow cast by my political labels. Eventually I devised a routine: The *Ramayana* is a verse epic, and I was determined that my translation should be in modern rhyming verse. But composing even trivial rhymes can often prove difficult. So each night, I would read the Sanskrit original carefully and translate it into Chinese prose. The next day, on my way to work, and in between all the phone calls and letters, I would turn the prose into verse. I often wrote out the prose in an illegible cursive and carried it in my pocket so that I could take it out in spare moments and mull over the rhymes. As I stared into space, no one could have known what I was thinking.

Outside the window, I could see the Asiatic apple trees and flowers in bloom.

## A MINOR EPISODE

The beautiful weather brought with it no change in my political status. I had resigned myself to living out my days quietly as a security guard, with no further political turmoil, but this was not to be.

One day, I noticed new big-character posters written on yellow paper, pasted onto the temporary bamboo stands outside my door. The posters were signed by several dozen lecturers in the department, and they denounced members of the May 16th Group. I ignored them at first, since there was always someone denouncing something. But then my curiosity got the better of me, and I was shocked to find that they were denouncing me: I was in fact suspected of having been part of the May 16th Group. This was absurd. Everyone knew that the ultra-leftist May 16th Group consisted of young people from good class backgrounds. I was neither young nor from a good class background, being neither a worker, farmer, nor a revolutionary cadre— in fact, I was just about as unlikely a candidate for the May 16th Group as could be. I should have just laughed and put the matter out of my mind, but I found myself unable to laugh or even snort in response, as I had when reading the poster attacking my essay "Springtime in Yanyuan." I don't know how the army thought propaganda team and revolutionary committee could have come up with such an improbable idea. Nor was that the only ludicrous thing about the whole affair: After the entire country had shouted its voice hoarse about May 16th, and a Jinggangshan leader had even publicly admitted that he belonged to the group, the mania evaporated quietly—it turned out that the May 16th Group didn't even exist. This was only one of the many absurd instances of chasing windmills that took place during the Cultural Revolution.

## A FARCE

Before long, it seemed that the Cultural Revolution had passed its peak, and the movement was drawing to a close. Although our motto was "Chaos confuses the enemy," our chaos had confused no one but ourselves. Now that things were slowly returning to normal, the most pressing task was to restore order within the Party ranks and iron out the irregularities, like the fact that a non-Party member from the workers' thought propaganda team worked for the Party branch.

Many ordinary Party members would have to reclaim their Party membership. Apart from the Gang of Four and their cronies, nearly all former members had been ousted at some point during the Cultural Revolution. There would be no Party that needed order restored if there were no Party members, so it was decreed that all former members would have to be officially reinstated via a process involving peer discussion and approval from Party superiors. This would be a huge project. After discussing the matter with the army-and-workers' thought propaganda team, the department leaders—including the worker who was not a Party member—decided to select one exemplary Party member whose reinstatement would serve as a model for all others. That person would have to be perfect in all respects, possess a high degree of political consciousness, and come from a faultless class background. Eventually they chose a man called Ma, the student I had chosen and mentored with an eye to his becoming my teaching assistant and eventual successor. Now that I was a capitalist counterrevolutionary academic authority, I would serve as a useful test of his Party loyalties. Ma came from a peasant family and was the son of a revolutionary martyr. His class background and our relationship made him the ideal choice.

One afternoon, those Party members of the department still on campus were summoned to the student cafeteria and told to bring a small wooden stool to sit on. When we arrived, we discovered that the long tables in the cafeteria had been pushed aside to make space for the wooden stools. On a large table at the front of the room lay some woolen pants among other clothing, a radio, which was still a luxury back then, and a few other odds and ends. I was too far back in the crowd to get a closer look at the things on the table. The bizarre assortment of objects reminded me of a flea market or yard sale. There was also a stack of printed and bound lecture notes. Puzzled, I sat there, unable to tell what the lecture notes and pants had to do with each other, or indeed what any of the items had to do with this man's readmission to the Party.

People filtered in, and it was time to start. The chairman said a few words about the purpose of these proceedings before inviting the candidate for reinstatement to step forward and say a few words. The model Party member rose and began to speak confidently. The subject of his talk was "I Will Not Be the Golden Paper Doll of the Capitalist Academic Authority." Golden paper dolls were buried with the dead in traditional Chinese funeral rites; as for the "academic authority," everyone in the audience knew he was referring to me. By then I was used to being the target of various meetings, though I hadn't expected to be featured in this one. I listened to this former student of mine denounce the sugar-coated bombs of the academic authority, and tell the story of how he had been poisoned by capitalist ideas into desiring bourgeois comforts and so on. When he described how close he had come to betraying his proletariat background, he nearly broke down and cried. He gestured at the things laid out on the table as though they were evidence of his narrow escape. Then he grew angry, picked up the bound lecture notes—

which turned out to be lectures on Sanskrit—and tore them down the middle. Scraps of paper fluttered to the ground like butterfly wings. "He'll go for the beautiful woolen pants or the radio next," I thought. But he only drew his hand back. Saved from destruction, the pants and radio glittered unscathed on the table. I was bewildered, as was the rest of the audience. The destruction of these capitalist trinkets was meant to be the climax of today's show; instead of generous applause, the man's performance earned a stunned silence.

Needless to say, the farce was a failure.

As we trudged back to Block 35, people were chattering: Why had Ma destroyed the Sanskrit lecture notes, which arguably had nothing to do with capitalism, rather than the fancy woolen pants, which were a perfect symbol of bourgeois pleasures? I, too, gave some thought to the story of this man, who had spent the past dozen years at Peking University. He was a consummate hypocrite: As a student, he had been extremely respectful, but another side of him came to light during the Cultural Revolution. For instance, it was extremely inappropriate to sign political banners with your own name, and only two people in the whole university insisted on doing it. Both, Ma included, happened to be in our department. That made him an object of ridicule for some time. When I first took part in a political study group at the university, I told him frankly that his behavior wasn't appropriate for the son of a revolutionary martyr or a member of the proletariat. Presumably, he never forgave me for saying that, which may explain his later behavior. I never found out how the rest of the department regained entry into the Party.

REGAINING PARTY MEMBERSHIP

Eventually, the university's project to reinstate all Party members was nearing completion, and only a few outsiders remained. I was one of them; my name must have been at the very bottom of the list.

One day, the department's Party branch officials summoned me to a meeting, and I knew that it was finally my turn. I had long been reassigned from my job as a security guard to the Hindi research center. The Party branch secretary and the army officer attached to our department told me that the authorities had decided not only to reinstate my salary but to repay the amount that had been docked from my salary. I was very touched. I decided then and there that I would donate the extra money to the national coffers, in lieu of unpaid Party membership fees. A colleague I respected gave me one thousand five hundred yuan, and told me that I could expect to receive another four or five thousand yuan. I gave the envelope containing my salary to the Party branch, unopened.

I don't remember whether there was a Party branch meeting on the question of reinstating my membership. But one day the head of the army thought propaganda team and the secretary of the department Party branch came to ask me: "Have you reflected on your errors?" I was at a loss for words. I certainly suffered from all kinds of personal faults, but I had never been involved in the Kuomintang or other counterrevolutionary organizations—I had no political errors worth speaking of. I stood there silently, until the officer finally changed the subject. Soon another cadre from the branch propaganda committee or the organization committee came to tell me that the branch had decided to restore my Party membership with two years' probation. I was livid. I had practically paid for my opposition to Nie Yuanzi with my life. I had been persecuted, imprisoned, and struggled against, and after surviving all of this I was now to receive two years' probation? Where was the justice in this? I was bitterly disappointed in the Party. The cadre saw the expression on my face and said that the branch could call a meeting to reopen my case for discussion. Enough, I thought. I couldn't bring myself to sign the notification letter with the word "agree," and I knew that writing "do not agree" would only be asking for trouble. I thought about it for a moment. "There's no need to call another meeting," I said to the cadre, and signed the letter with the words "basically agree." "You know what the word 'basically' means," I told him. Then I thought: Is a Party member on probation worthy of donating his salary to the national coffers? So I kept the four or five thousand yuan I had been planning to donate.

Now that my Party membership was restored, was I truly, fully liberated? There is nothing more to say, the chapter must come to an end. My experience of the Cultural Revolution was over and my story draws to a close.

# FURTHER REFLECTIONS

BUT WITH FURTHER thought I must continue—I must not stop here.

During the sixteen or so years since the Cultural Revolution ended, I've been thinking constantly about what it all meant. While writing this memoir, I've been able to think long and hard about this, and I offer here some of my reflections.

First, have we learned from history?

The Cultural Revolution was neither cultural nor revolutionary: Everyone agrees that it was nothing but a ten-year-long disaster. The country suffered incalculable losses, both intellectually and economically. But now that we've paid sizable sums in tuition fees, what do we have to show for it? We haven't yet learned our money's worth.

I believe that the Cultural Revolution can serve as an excellent example of what not to do; reflecting on it will show us, by extension, how to act in the future. This is of crucial importance in helping our country to move forward. If we don't learn from it, we will have missed an unprecedented opportunity.

Some people say that what's past is past, and there's no need to waste time rehashing it. This leads to my next question: Is the Cultural Revolution a thing of the past?

We are materialists, and seeking truth from facts lies at the heart of materialism. If we are serious about seeking truth, we must admit that the Cultural Revolution is not merely a thing of the past. Look carefully. Ask anyone who was implicated, especially any of the older generation of intellectuals who were persecuted then, and you will learn, if they are forthright with you, of much lingering resentment. Young people, on the other hand, hardly know anything about the Cultural Revolution, which is little more than a fairy tale to them. This troubles me: If they barely know what happened, who can guarantee that they won't make the same mistakes themselves? I cannot speak for all intellectuals, but of the older generation I can guarantee that the very mention of the Cultural Revolution is enough to awaken a simmering bitterness.

The older Party cadres who were persecuted may not harbor bitterness to the same degree, being the unselfish, politically conscious citizens that they are. Despite their devotion to establishing the new China, many of them were also struggled against in the Cultural Revolution, but I know few cadres personally, so I cannot judge how they feel. Yet I am reminded of a brief but telling encounter that I would like to share here. In 1978, when the Chinese People's Political Consultative Conference started up again, I ran into an elderly Party cadre at the Beijing Friendship Hotel. He was a long-standing Communist who was very well known in literary and artistic circles. Before the Cultural Revolution, we had both been members of the social science working group at the conference, but we hadn't seen each other in more than a decade. His first words to me were: "It used to be said that 'the scholar can be killed, but he cannot be humiliated.' The Cultural Revolution proved that not only can the scholar be killed but he can also be humiliated." He began to roar with laughter, but there were tears in his eyes. I couldn't even smile with him. Surely this man must have suffered untold anguish.[1]

He was not alone; I, for one, also felt humiliated, and I imagine that many others must have as well. We Chinese intellectuals are descended from a tradition of scholars who would rather be killed than humiliated, a tradition that makes us overly sensitive, perhaps more so than our counterparts in other countries.

This encounter led me to consider the history and present status of intellectuals in China. In Chinese feudal society, intellectuals didn't constitute a social class, but scholars would have ranked ahead of farmers, artisans, and merchants, being at neither the very top nor the very bottom of the feudal system. They commanded respect. I was born too late to have known intellectuals like those in the Qing dynasty novel *The Scholars*.[2] But I did know a few university professors of the warlord and Kuomintang era. They were well respected and well paid, and as social status often determines an individual's consciousness, many of them were self-assured, cocky types. By the time I became a professor, Kuomintang influence was waning, and soaring inflation left professors with a pitiful income. Yet many of them still wore the long scholars' gowns that indicated their social status.

I, like many other professors, greeted the Communist Liberation of 1949 enthusiastically. For once, we were proud to be Chinese, and as excited and naïve as young children. We saw "blue skies in the liberated areas," as a popular song of the time went. Everything seemed to glow with promise.

But the glow didn't last long. In the Three-Antis and Five-Antis Campaigns, our first major criticism campaigns, I "bathed in a medium-size tub," as we said at the time, which consisted in making a public confession at a department meeting.[3] I came away feeling lighter, stronger, as though I had been cleansed of filth. Such were the thrills of thought reform. But the criticism campaigns rushed by, and before long I could barely keep up. We criticized Wu Xun. We criticized Redology, we criticized Hu Feng, we criticized Hu Shi...there was no end to these campaigns, which culminated in the Anti-Rightist Movement of 1957.[4] Although I had not been assigned any class labels or political "hats," I was always anxious and on edge—those were unhappy days. But at the time, I had no misgivings about the mass campaigns. I went to criticism meetings every day and read all the relevant material. Incidentally, the airplane position had not been invented yet, so public criticism meetings were not the great spectacles that they became during the Cultural Revolution. Although I was puzzled to notice that the whims of the crowd were difficult to reconcile with Mao's original directives, I never doubted Mao's famous words: "If the Anti-Rightist Movement is a conspiracy, it is a conspiracy in broad daylight."

The flood of campaigns didn't stop with the Anti-Rightist Movement. By the Lushan Conference of 1959, extreme leftism had already reached its climax, but the conference led only to another campaign in the Anti-Rightist Movement. In the three years of famine that followed, I and other intellectuals endured starvation without question or complaint. Indeed, the whole citizenry remained resolute, such is the unsurpassed resilience of Chinese intellectuals and the Chinese people.

The Cultural Revolution, which began in 1966, was a necessary development of this earlier radicalization. After the revolution, a colleague in my department who had been part of New Beida told me that I wouldn't have been persecuted if I had not been rash enough to speak up against the Empress Dowager. I got what was coming to me: Everything I owned was confiscated, and I was beaten, yelled at, struggled against, imprisoned, and nearly killed. But while I regretted it then, I am now glad I had a chance to experience the revolution— missing out on such a spectacle would truly be a cause for regret.

I observed many things and thought many things while I was in the cowshed. And I gradually began to question why the intellectuals had been singled out. It is true we had many faults, but our accusers were not perfect. I didn't know then what I know now, so my doubts remained superficial. But instead of blaming other people, such as those who instigated the revolution, I became intensely introspective. To borrow a Christian concept, I became overwhelmed by guilt.

Whether other intellectuals felt the same way I do not know, but the effects of guilt on me were real. Before 1949, I had assumed that everything about politics was tainted and had made up my mind to avoid it. I knew little about the Communists, but I could see that the Kuomintang government was corrupt and would have to be overthrown. As I've said, the feverish self-criticism of the post-1949 political campaigns changed my attitude. I realized that not all political activity was tainted; the Communist Party, for instance, was motivated by genuine ideals. I also blamed myself for having selfishly pursued my own academic career thousands of miles away while my people were dying in battle against the Japanese. My scholarship, my scraps of erudition, if they could even be called that, were a source of shame to me. For a long time, I called myself a fruit-reaper, a parasite who had contributed nothing to my country but returned to pluck the fruit of victory. I wondered how I would ever make amends.

I fantasized that another war against Japan would give me a chance to prove myself. I knew I was capable of fighting, of sacrifice. I devoured novels about World War II and about the Chinese civil war. I worshipped the soldiers and Communists they depicted, vowing to emulate their heroism. I threw myself eagerly into these childish fantasies.

I had formerly despised personality cults. Before the war, I used to sneer at Kuomintang supporters for worshipping Chiang Kai-shek. As a student at Tsinghua University, I had met Chiang when we marched to Nanjing after the Mukden Incident and requested an audience with him. He had lied to us and we resented him for it. My former teacher, Mr. Chen Yinke, felt the same way about this man, as he wrote in a poem, "One who delights in flowers is saddened to climb high towers."[5] Later, I moved to Germany during World War II, when the fascist cult of Hitler was at its height. The frequent use of the greeting "Heil Hitler!" puzzled me. A pretty teenage girl once told me, "Bearing a child of Hitler's would be the greatest honor of my life!" I found the Hitler cult incomprehensible. I couldn't help thinking: We Chinese people would never fall for a personality cult like that.

I returned to China after the war, and three years later, the country was liberated by the Communists from Kuomintang rule. Many other intellectuals of my generation shared in the euphoria. Each year there were two grand parades at Tiananmen Square, on Labor Day and on National Day, which commemorated the founding of the People's Republic. We always got up at dawn and assembled on the main campus of Peking University to march to a narrow lane near the Dongdan crossing. We would wait there for hours. When the parade began officially at ten, our company would march through Tiananmen to be inspected by the Great Leader. At the time, the three large gates to the square had not yet been demolished, and east of the gates, it was impossible to see either the main Tiananmen gate or the leaders. But once we had turned the corner past the gates, we could see the Great Leader, so the crowd, thousands strong, would begin to chant: "Long live Chairman Mao!" At first the phrase "Long live" stuck in my throat. But before long, because of my natural aptitude in crowd behavior, I too found myself shouting at the top of my voice, as though these words were the cry of my soul. I had fallen under the Great Leader's spell.

This is an honest account of my intellectual journey. If the existence of oceans can be inferred from a drop of water, or the universe from a grain of sand, then it may be true that other intellectuals at that time acted in a simlar way. If nothing else, our ordeals demonstrate that Chinese intellectuals, both old and young, are consumed with love for our country. For centuries, our intellectual heritage has been deeply rooted in patriotism: This is a distinctive trait that makes us different from intellectuals in other countries.

"Who has realized that life is but a dream?" the military strategist Zhuge Liang asks in Luo Guanzhong's fourteenth-century novel *Ro-*

*mance of the Three Kingdoms*. And he continues, "I have known this all my life." Unlike Zhuge Liang, I am not adept at seeing through the waking dream that is life. Even after I had been imprisoned, I continued to support the Cultural Revolution. But then I discovered that, as the Western saying goes, "All that glitters is not gold." While in the cowshed, I met some of the soldiers and workers who had been sent to support the leftist faction at Peking University, the former objects of my infatuation. "All citizens must learn from the People's Liberation Army!" "The proletariat must take the lead in everything!" I had believed in and obeyed all these slogans. But upon actually meeting these soldiers and workers, I realized that some of them were arrogant thugs who knew nothing about politics. I immediately came to my senses. To be sure, no one is perfect. But I never imagined that the objects of my worship would act so despicably. As materialists, we should be transparent and pragmatic; we cannot deceive ourselves. I must say that although we intellectuals had our faults, we cannot have been the worst offenders.

After all my ramblings I want to emphasize that the persecution of intellectuals during the Cultural Revolution was unreasonable, indeed indefensible. For the vast majority of those who were persecuted, it is not a thing of the past. For myself, I suppose I am glad to have had an unforgettable experience in the cowshed. But even now that my paltry successes have surrounded me with a cacophony of flattering voices, I sometimes think: I should have committed suicide. That I did not do so is a stain on my character; my very existence is cause for shame; I am living on borrowed time. I know such thoughts can lead to no good. But I can't deny these thoughts and I may as well record it here.

This brings me to my third question: Have the victims of the revolution given voice to their bitterness? Evidently not.

To answer this question fully, I must return to 1949. I have already written about the emotional state in which I and other intellectuals found ourselves; I would like to add a note on the Chinese diaspora. Chinese living overseas felt the Liberation of the motherland as a seismic change in their own lives. The diasporic communities seemed quite patriotic, and as patriotism peaked in 1949, scores of young people braved the grueling and dangerous journey home. Like the native intellectuals, they were willing to dedicate their lives to China's progress. Many Chinese scholars gave up superior living standards and research conditions overseas to return to China. Among them was Lao She, the prominent novelist and playwright who later took his own life during the Cultural Revolution. They were all proud of their country and full of optimism, seeing a bright future for China and for themselves.

Then the mood shifted, extreme leftist thinking took over, and the diasporic intellectuals' overseas connections became an excuse for persecuting them. Even a child can see that someone who used to live abroad of course retains friends and connections from that time. Our supposedly leftist leaders seized on this argument to label people as special agents or foreign spies. No one was safe. The Cultural Revolution only made things worse. How many upright, patriotic people were wrongly accused? Some were persecuted to death. Those who were still alive hurried to leave China. They had fought to return and were now fighting to leave. I myself witnessed many such cases. Anyone with half a brain would realize what a loss this was to our country. These intellectuals were sad to leave China, like any child who has to leave his parents. But many felt they had no choice but to flee.

Of the intellectuals who stayed as well as those who didn't, who has given voice to their bitterness?

A brand of so-called scar literature concerning the Cultural Revolution emerged some years ago. As far as I can tell, the authors of these books were young people who cannot be said to have many "scars," while those whose scars are deepest have chosen, for their own reasons, not to vent their outrage. This suppression of the past cannot be ignored; it threatens to endanger China's progress.

Today we stress the importance of social harmony, without which the economy cannot grow, and politics cannot fulfill its intended function. But while many intellectuals, and older intellectuals in particular, are still filled with resentment, the true unity and harmony we need has not been achieved.

Although intellectuals still harbor bitterness, earn a pitiful salary, and cannot help grumbling sometimes, they are genuinely loyal and as patriotic as ever. Yet someone prominent recently said, in light of the dissolution of the Soviet Union: "Chinese intellectuals are no more than hairs on the skin of imperialism." These words are only hearsay, of course, but the reports may be true. Does the person who said this have the slightest conscience? His words are troubling.

If one of his kind gains political power, no intellectuals will be left standing.

My final question is: What made the Cultural Revolution possible?

This is a complicated question that I am ill-equipped to answer; the only people in a position to tackle it refuse to do so and do not seem to want anyone else to try. I think their refusal runs contrary to the attitude of truth-seeking that a materialist should have. If we were to address this question seriously, the whole country—including, of course, the intellectuals—would be deeply grateful. They would put aside their baggage and march on ahead, working collectively toward the harmony and progress of our socialist society.

If we refuse to study this problem, we leave it to foreigners to continue to do so. As Confucius put it: "If ritual propriety has been lost at court, seek it in the villages." Some foreigners are studying the facts objectively and reaching solid conclusions. Regardless of whether their work addresses the most crucial issues, honesty is better than lies. But others harbor ulterior motives. They muddy the waters, spreading rumors and false accusations. Though they are like "ants trying to move trees," as the saying goes, and though it is unlikely that their warped version of events will influence anything, it can lead to no good.

Where have we come from, and where are we going? I believe that the issues are clear. These are my thoughts and my ramblings come to a close.

# Author's Afterword

I WORKED INTERMITTENTLY on a first draft of this book between March 4, 1988, and April 5, 1989, but only this spring was I seized by the desire to copy out a final manuscript. Today is June 3rd, and it has taken me about three months to nearly complete a revision of the first draft.

I originally told myself that I would simply write an objective account of what happened, without bitterness or rancor. But I am, after all, a human being with emotions, and I found it impossible to avoid tears and outrage as I was writing; I felt I needed to accept these emotions as part of the story if I wanted to be true to my experience. The largest difference between the first and final draft is that there are fewer tears and less outrage in this version. I would have preferred the original version, but I decided to tone down my writing in order to avoid stepping on people's toes.

A careful reader will be able to tell that there are three kinds of characters mentioned in this book: some are anonymous, some are referred to by surname, and only a few people are referred to by their full names. In the first two cases, I have elected to preserve the privacy of the individuals concerned; only where I am convinced that certain individuals pose a threat to our socialist society do I record their names as a warning to others.

In the years since the Cultural Revolution, I have never taken revenge on any of these people, even though my position as department
head was restored and I was named to national political positions. I
could have made life difficult for my former enemies, and I hope the
individuals alluded to in this book understand that I have written it
as a purely historical document. I continue to value the relationships
we were able to build before and after the Cultural Revolution.

I have written a total of about eight million characters in my lifetime, about 70 percent of which were written after the Cultural Revolution. Had I succeeded in my attempt to commit suicide at the
time, none of these works would have been written. Was surviving
the revolution a stroke of good or ill fortune? Even now, I cannot say
I know the answer to that question.

—JI XIANLIN
*June 3, 1992*

# Appendix: My Heart Is a Mirror

I WAS BORN too late to witness the beginning of the twentieth century. But in seven years' time, I will have lived to see the beginning of the twenty-first. My physical and mental health suggests that there is no reason I shouldn't survive to see that day. Being nearly contemporaneous with the past century, I think I qualify to write an essay entitled "China in the Twentieth Century and I."

Each person's heart is a mirror reflecting the changing times, and mine is no exception. I consider myself to be quite an observant person, and the reflections in my mirror may not be the most detailed impressions of historical events, but they are not the cloudiest. I believe that my memories accurately reflect ninety years of twentieth-century history.

I was born in 1911, in the year of the revolution that overthrew the Qing dynasty: Two months and four days after I was born, the last emperor lost his seat on the Dragon Throne. I sometimes joke that I am a closet royalist. One of my earliest memories is of villagers speaking of the "imperial court" in tones of awe long after the Qing dynasty had crumbled. I had no idea what the court was. As for the emperor, he seemed to be both god and man, an extremely powerful animal.

That was the reflection of the dying Qing dynasty in my heart's mirror.

My hometown is in Qingping County, which is now part of the city of Linqing, well known for being one of the poorest parts of Shandong. I was born into a family of penniless subsistence farmers. My grandparents died before I was born, so I never met them and never experienced a grandfather's love. They left three sons, of whom my father was the eldest, and the seventh eldest male among his cousins. The youngest of my uncles, who was orphaned almost from birth, was given to another family and surnamed Diao from then on. The two remaining brothers, my father and uncle, were alone with no one in the world they could rely on. They were penniless and constantly hungry. When the hunger became too overwhelming, they would go to the jujube woods and eat rotting jujubes from the ground. I don't know much about this period of their life, because neither of them spoke of it—perhaps it was so harrowing that they were unwilling to reawaken old memories or to leave their children with images of such grim poverty.

The two brothers would starve if they stayed in the village, so they decided to try their luck in the big city and find a way of surviving there. The nearest city was Jinan, the capital of Shandong, where they were simple country bumpkins who didn't know a soul. Possibly for the same reasons, they never spoke of their difficulties during this time, and I never asked about them.

My uncle, the younger of the two, was eventually able to eke out a living in Jinan, surviving by the skin of his teeth like a blade of grass among the rocks. The brothers agreed that my uncle would stay in Jinan where he could earn money, and my father would return home to become a farmer. They hoped that my uncle would make a name for himself. That way, even if he didn't become rich, people would respect him, and he would win honor for himself and their father and mother.

But being a farmer requires land, and their family had no land. My father somehow managed to survive and even started a family. Perhaps my grandfather had left him half an acre of land. Again, I don't know exactly how he scraped by.

I was born not long after the god of fortune smiled on my family for the first time. My uncle had lost his job and had been roaming around Guandong. With his last coin, he bought a ticket in a lottery raising funds for flood relief in Hubei. He won the jackpot, apparently worth thousands of taels of silver. Our family was suddenly rich. My father bought ten acres of well-irrigated land, and to show off their newfound riches, the brothers decided to have a large house built. Since there weren't enough bricks to be had at short notice, my father announced to the village that if anyone was willing to tear his own house down and sell him the bricks, he would pay several times the going rate for them. Sure enough, his extravagant offer attracted takers, and while other families dismantled their houses, we built ours. It was a large courtyard house with five rooms in each of the north, west, and east wings, and an impressive, south-facing entrance. The brothers had finally done well for themselves.

But their good fortune didn't last long. My father was generous to a fault. On a whim, when he was going to market in another village, he might treat everyone there to lunch. Before long, he had to sell the land and tear down two wings of the new house so that the bricks and tiles could be sold off. The bricks he had bought for their weight in gold were now being sold for next to nothing.

The reverie was over; we were penniless again.

By the time I was old enough to remember anything, we were destitute. We could only afford to eat wheat congee about twice a year, and our diet consisted mostly of sorghum cakes; even cornmeal cakes were a treat. In the spring and summer, I would cut and bundle grass or sorghum leaves, and take them to my second cousin's home to feed his cow. Then I would hang around until he gave me a meal of cornmeal cakes. In the summer and autumn, my two aunts, who lived across from us, would take me with them to glean wheat and beans in the fields of neighboring villages. I would return with a small handful of grain to give to my mother. After many such trips, the wheat could eventually be ground into enough flour for a meal of wheat congee, the greatest delicacy I could imagine. My mother never ate a single bite. She simply sat watching me eat, her eyes growing wet. At the time I was naturally unable to understand her feelings. I decided then that when I grew up, I would buy her wheat congee. Yet in the poet's words, "Just as the tree longs for stillness when the wind blows, the child longs to take care of his parents when they are no longer there." My mother passed away before I ever had the chance to treat her to a meal of wheat congee, a loss that I grieve and regret to this day.

In my father's generation, there were eleven men in the family. Six of them left for Guandong because they were unable to make a living in the village and were never heard from again. Of the five who were left, one was given to another family as a child. My eldest uncle had a son whom I never met because he died young. That made me the only male child of the family in my generation, and in traditional Chinese society, that was no small thing. My uncle, who lived in Jinan, only had one daughter, so he and my father decided that I should be sent to Jinan. I was too young to understand how my mother must have felt. Many years later, I was told that she had apparently said, "If only I'd known he would never come back, I would have died rather than let him leave!" I never heard her say those words, but they have echoed in my mind over the decades. As the poet Meng Jiao wrote, comparing a child's debt to his parents to a plant's debt to the sun, "How can a blade of grass repay the warmth of the spring?"

I left home when I was six.

Life has its ironies, and no one chooses the life they lead. If I had stayed in the village, I would have remained a peasant all my life. It would have been a hard life, but one with few hazards. Instead, I saw the world, learned many things, learned about life, and made something of a name for myself. The path has been easy at times and uphill at others, and now I have grown old. If I had been permitted to choose my own path in advance, which life would I have chosen? That would not have been an easy choice.

The reflection in my heart's mirror when I left home was of a once-wealthy village family whose fortunes had crumbled and fallen on hard times.

Jinan was a new world. I had never seen mountains before, and I had pictured them as gigantic stone pillars. I was fascinated by the sight of real mountains.

My uncle took great pains to give me a good education since I was the only male descendant of the Ji family. After about a year of traditional Chinese school, which consisted in learning to recite the classics, I was sent to one of the new primary schools, Jinan Teacher Training Institute No. 1 Primary School. The educational reforms advocated by the May Fourth Movement had reached Shandong, and the principal of the school was a reform-minded man who instituted the use of a modern textbook. My uncle caught sight of the chapter containing "The Camel and the Arab," a translated fable, and cried, "That's ridiculous—everyone knows camels don't talk! We'll have to put you in a different school!" So I was sent to the New Education School instead. Transferring to my new school turned out to be a straightforward process. There were no strings to pull or bribes to pay, and I was simply interviewed by a teacher who wrote the character for "donkey" on the board. I could identify the character, whereas my cousin, a year older than me, couldn't. I was hence put in the lowest class of the upper school, while he was put in the highest class of the lower school. A single arbitrarily chosen character had given me a year's advantage over him. Our first textbooks were in classical Chinese, but we soon switched to modern Chinese books, in which even the toads and tortoises had speaking parts, not to mention the camels. This time, my uncle didn't intervene.

My uncle was an extremely intelligent man who had never received a formal education. He had somehow taught himself to write poems and lyrics, practice calligraphy, and cut seals by hand. He had also read widely in classical Chinese and was fascinated by Song and Ming dynasty neo-Confucianist philosophy, an extraordinary interest for an uneducated man. To this day, I can see him sitting up straight at his desk, reading Qing dynasty philosophical compendia such as the *Wang Qing Jing Jie*, looking completely and absurdly serious.

My uncle's philosophy shaped my education. He wanted me to receive a classical education as his brother's son and the bearer of the family name so that I would pass my learning on to subsequent generations of the Ji family. I was forbidden to read Ming dynasty novels such as *Dream of the Red Chamber*, *Romance of the Three Kingdoms*, or *The Water Margin*, because he considered them frivolous. But I enjoyed reading novels precisely because they were forbidden and devoured dozens of them. After school, I would hide behind heaps of bricks and tiles and read instead of going home, or read under the covers with a flashlight. I spent years immersed in these novels.

My uncle had other plans for my education. Throughout my time at Zhengyi Middle School, he paid for me to be tutored in classical Chinese, and in my lessons we read difficult and obscure texts such as the long history *Chronicle of Zuo*. After having dinner at home, I would immediately set off for the Shangshi English Learning Society, where I took English lessons until late in the night. Several years of my childhood passed this way.

The motto of the late Qing dynasty reformers was that "Chinese learning is to serve as the foundation, and Western learning is to be applied." My uncle certainly believed in the first half of the motto, but it was hard to say whether he also believed in the second. At the time, many people thought that acquiring some Western knowledge could help secure a government job and make you rich. They could see that foreign learning was useful, even if they didn't appreciate it in itself. But my uncle was not given to pandering to foreigners, and he never doubted the superiority of Chinese civilization.

Upon finishing middle school in 1926, I was accepted to the humanities program of the Affiliated High School of Shandong University in Beiyuan Baihezhuang. My teachers there were all extremely erudite men. They included Mr. Wang Kunyu, the Chinese teacher; Mr. You Tong, Mr. Liu, and Mr. Yang, the English teachers; Mr. Wang, who taught mathematics; Mr. Qi Yunpu, who taught history and geography; Mr. Ju Simin, who taught ethics and was also the principal of Zhengyi Middle School; and Mr. Wanyan Xiangqing, the principal of No. 1 Middle School. Of the two teachers of Chinese classics, one was nicknamed Empire of the Great Qing (I no longer remember his name), and another was a Hanlin Academy scholar under dynastic rule. Neither of them ever had to bring a book to their classes on the *Book of Documents*, *I Ching*, and *Classic of Poetry*, because they already knew the texts by heart. They were excellent teachers, and the campus itself was filled with lotus ponds and willows, which made it an excellent environment for studying.

I have always been easily influenced by my environment, which explains why it was only in high school that I began to study hard. While I was a relatively good student in elementary and middle school, I never was and never aspired to be the best student in my class. I was content to keep fishing and catching prawns. As a high school student, I was at the top of the class in English, and my teacher, Mr. Wang Kunyu, often commended my essays. Doing well in other classes wasn't difficult as long as I was willing to learn the material by heart. For the first time in my life, I had the highest grades in my class, and my 95 percent average was, in fact, the highest in the school. The president of Shandong University at the time was Wang Shoupeng, the minister of education for Shandong Province, who had previously been a primus or top scorer in the imperial examinations. He gave me a fan he had inscribed with poetry and a pair of scrolls with a rhyming couplet. The recognition spurred me on and doing well in exams became a point of pride for me. My hard work paid off; I was first in the class in midterms and finals four times in two years.

At the time, China was overrun by competing warlords, and the balance of power was shifting constantly. In 1924, the dominant Zhili faction was defeated in a coup by the pro-Japanese Fengtian clique. One year the high school students were invited to Shandong University's annual ceremony honoring Confucius, and there I saw Zhang Zhongchang, a general belonging to the Fengtian clique, who had more cash, concubines, and soldiers under his command than he knew what to do with. I have never forgotten the sight of him in the long robes of traditional dress, kowtowing in front of the shrine to Confucius.

In 1928, Chiang Kai-shek launched a military campaign to unify China in the name of "revolution" and Sun Yat-sen's legacy. His Northern Expedition gained momentum and won the Communists' support as he marched north from Guangdong to Jinan. Japanese forces attempted to take advantage of the confusion by sending troops to Jinan, sparking a violent conflict that resulted in thousands of civilian casualties on both the Chinese and Japanese sides. Schools in Jinan closed as a result.

At this time, the reflections in my heart's mirror were of an education that blended elements of both the traditional and the modern approaches, against the backdrop of constant fighting between warlords.

The Kuomintang army retreated, and the Japanese eventually succeeded in occupying Jinan. Schools did not reopen, and for the next year I belonged to a conquered race.

The Japanese were now the only authorities in Jinan. Like all illegitimate rulers, despite their outward show of strength, they were actually terrified of the Chinese people and treated ordinary civilians as dangerous enemies. They often conducted lightning raids of civilian houses, and news that the Japanese were coming always caused commotion at home. Some of us felt that we should open the main door, while others thought we should close it. The former pictured the Japanese soldiers saying, "How dare you be so bold as to leave your door wide open!" and then stabbing us to death. The latter pictured the Japanese soldiers saying, "You must have sinister designs, or why would you close your door instead of opening it to welcome the Imperial Army?" and then stabbing us to death. We vacillated endlessly between leaving the door open and closing it. Everyone was frantic. Our terror of the Japanese could not be imagined by an outsider.

I knew the Japanese hated students for having started the movement to burn Japanese goods in Shandong. Since schools were closed, I shaved my head in an attempt to pass as a shop apprentice. One day, as I was walking along Dongmen Street, a few Japanese soldiers came toward us and began to search everyone on the street. I knew I had to stay calm; if I tried to run I would be killed. I tried to look nonchalant as I walked up to the soldier, who searched me and found that I was wearing a belt. He was pleased with his discovery: "Very cunning you. You not apprentice, you student. Apprentice don't tie belt!" He gave me a blow to the head with his cudgel, but luckily I didn't faint. I immediately started explaining that these days, lowly apprentices were also paid well enough to afford belts. The soldier refused to believe me. Just as we were arguing, another soldier came up, possibly one who was higher ranked than the one I had been arguing with. I broke out in a sweat. "Just let him go!" he said irritably with a wave of his hand. I quickly made my escape.

During this year, my heart's mirror reflected my life as a member of a conquered people.

In 1929, the Japanese troops retreated, and the Kuomintang re-took Jinan. A new stage of my schooling began. The high school I had been attending was closed. I was permitted to enroll at the new Jinan Government High School, the only high school in the province, without having to take an entrance examination.

There were now quite a few Kuomintang officials on the faculty. The ideological tone on campus became more pronounced, and the Kuomintang bias irritated me. The educational philosophy of the school had also shifted, most notably in Chinese classes. The teacher nicknamed Empire had left, classical Chinese was no longer taught, and essays were to be written in modern instead of classical Chinese. Many of the new teachers were prominent intellectuals in the May Fourth Movement. My first Chinese teacher at the new school was Mr. Hu Yepin, who would later die for the Communist cause. Mr. Hu seldom followed a fixed syllabus. Instead, he spoke with great urgency about contemporary literature and art and about a new "literature of the people"—that is, the literature of the proletariat. Several of us responded to these ideas enthusiastically, setting up tables outside the dormitories and inviting our fellow students to study sessions on the subject. We were even going to publish a journal, for which I wrote an essay called "The Task of Contemporary Literature" that I had cobbled together from chunks of Marxist aesthetic theory translated from the Japanese. The translation was scarcely intelligible, but it was full of zeal and revolutionary slogans in equal measure. At the time, Mr. Hu was wanted by the Kuomintang, and he fled to Shanghai before my essay could be published. He was killed by the Kuomintang a couple of years later. My revolutionary zeal waned, and I had no further thoughts of revolution until the Communist Liberation in 1949.

Mr. Dong Qiufang took over from Mr. Hu as our Chinese teacher. He was a graduate of Peking University and friend of Lu Xun, who wrote the introduction to an anthology of Russian revolutionary literature translated by Dong. Mr. Dong commended my essays. He considered me the most talented writer in the class, indeed in the whole school, which naturally flattered me. For the past sixty years, I have maintained the habit of writing essays alongside my academic work. Regardless of their literary quality, they provide an outlet for my anger and joys and allow me to express my emotions and my ideals. I will always remember Mr. Dong with affection.

That year, the reflection in my heart's mirror was of a new stage in life.

After graduating in the summer of 1930, I traveled to Beijing along with most of my classmates to take the entrance examinations for universities there. All kinds of universities existed in Beijing at the time—state-run universities, private ones, religious ones—and they varied immensely in quality. The most prestigious among them were the two state-run universities, Peking University and Tsinghua University. We all applied to these two universities, which had dozens of students competing for each place. Being accepted to one of these extremely selective universities was considered a great honor, like being a proverbial carp transformed into a dragon. The year that I applied in Beijing, a fellow student from Shandong who was also traveling to Beijing told us that he had already taken the examinations five times; this was his sixth. He was rejected yet again. Suffering a nervous breakdown, he wandered around near Xi Mountain for seven days before recovering his senses. He decided to give up applying to university and go home, and I never learned what became of him.

Of course, I too applied to Peking University and Tsinghua, but unlike my friends, I didn't apply anywhere else. I must have seemed confident of getting in, but the truth was that I hadn't thought very hard about where to apply. My friends applied to an assortment of good, bad, and mediocre universities—some of them applied to seven or eight altogether. I've taken countless examinations over the course of a lifetime and have often been lucky. This was no exception. Both universities accepted me, and my friends envied the difficult choice I had before me.

I weighed my options for some time before settling on Tsinghua. Opportunities to study abroad were as highly sought after then as they are now, and Tsinghua was reputed to have the edge when it came to sending its students abroad. Since that was my eventual goal, I chose to enroll in Tsinghua's Western Literature Department (later renamed the Foreign Literature Department).

Tsinghua's Western Literature Department was well known at the time for having a faculty that consisted almost entirely of foreigners and for teaching in the original languages. Even the Chinese professors often conducted their classes in foreign languages, usually in English. This alone made it extremely attractive. It turned out that our foreign professors were mediocre scholars, many of whom would have barely qualified to teach high school in their native countries, and most of my required classes were unilluminating. But there were two especially memorable classes: I audited Mr. Chen Yinke's class on Buddhist literature in translation, and as an elective I chose Mr. Zhu Guangqian's class on the psychology of literature and art, which was effectively a class on aesthetics. Mr. Ye Gongchao of my own department taught us English in my first year. His English was fluent, but his ostentatiously unkempt appearance left me with a bad impression. I also remember Mr. Wu Mi's classes on the comparative study of Chinese and English poetry and on English Romantic poets.

I audited or sneaked into many classes in other departments. Mr. Zhu Ziqing, the renowned poet and essayist, was a professor of Chinese literature; Mr. Yu Pingbo taught Redology, the study of *Dream of the Red Chamber*; Ms. Xie Wanying, better known by the pen name Bing Xin, as well as Mr. Zheng Zhenduo, who wrote under the name Xi Di, also taught at Tsinghua. On one occasion, Ms. Xie courteously asked several male students, myself included, to leave her classroom. Although we failed in our attempt to attend that class, we were permitted to sit in on Mr. Zheng's lectures. Mr. Zheng was less arrogant than some of the other professors, and he had no patience for academic cliques. Wu Zuxiang, Lin Geng, Li Changzhi, and I were among the young students who got to know him by auditing his lectures. Along with Ba Jin and Jin Yi, he edited the avant-garde *Literary Quarterly,* and he permitted some of us to write or edit. We were thrilled to see our own names in print on the cover of the quarterly, and all of us remained friends with Mr. Zheng until his untimely death in a plane accident in 1958, which grieves me to this day.

The political situation at this time was tense. While Chiang Kai-shek was focused on eradicating the Communists, the Japanese army had entered Gubeikou and Manchuria. After the Mukden Incident, the staged attack on a Japanese railway that gave the Japanese an excuse to invade Manchuria, I joined a group of Tsinghua students protesting Chiang's refusal to declare war on Japan. In a rush of patriotism, we staged demonstrations and hunger strikes, and even traveled to Nanjing to present our demands. But Chiang deceived us, and we returned home without having succeeded in causing any change.

Tsinghua itself was not insulated from political turmoil. There was a deep rift between Kuomintang and Communist students. Comrade Hu Qiaomu, a history student in my class who would later become a prominent cadre, was already heavily involved in revolutionary work. It was an open secret that he slipped Communist pamphlets into our washbasins overnight. I remember one evening when he sat on my bed until late, attempting to persuade me to join him, but I was too timid and cautious. Instead, to repay his friendship, I agreed to help teach at the night school that he ran for workers' children.

The Communist and Kuomintang supporters among the students often clashed, but I knew little about their arguments since I wasn't involved in politics and had no interested in getting involved. I had leftist sympathies but wasn't affiliated with either camp. Communist and Kuomintang students did sometimes work together: For instance, many students traveled to villages near Shahe and Qinghe, to educate the villagers on the importance of resisting the Japanese. I took part in some of those trips, and remember seeing Kuomintang supporters there. After all, nearly all of us were patriots, in the long-standing patriotic tradition of Chinese intellectuals, even though Chiang Kai-shek was refusing to resist the Japanese invasion.

My family was still struggling financially. Whenever I was about to return to campus after the winter and summer breaks, I had trouble scraping together the funds to pay for tuition and board. As a state university, Tsinghua required minimal expense. Tuition was a nominal forty yuan a semester, and at graduation the university returned all tuition to students to subsidize the traditional post-graduation vacation. Rooms in the dormitories were free; board was six yuan a month and included meat at every meal. Even so, I could barely afford my studies. I must have been the only student from Qingping County attending a state university, so the county contributed fifty yuan a year toward my expenses. I also wrote a few articles as a way of earning some money to lighten my family's financial burden. I survived four years of university education that way, and at the end of the four years, I had a photograph taken in a rented graduation cap to mark the conclusion of my undergraduate career.

It was said that "graduation is unemployment," and none of my classmates were immune to what we called "the problem of finding a rice bowl" except the few children of wealthy magnates and high-ranking officials. By my third year, I began to worry about finding a job, especially since I would be my family's main breadwinner. I had no connections or talent for flattery. I spent sleepless nights worrying, but there was nothing to be done.

Just as I was about to graduate in the early summer of 1934, the principal of my alma mater in Jinan, Mr. Song Huanwu, sent word inviting me to return to the school as a Chinese teacher. My monthly salary would be 160 yuan, twice the salary of a university teaching assistant. Perhaps because I had published a few articles, I was considered a writer, and back then people assumed that a writer must be able to teach Chinese. I was overjoyed to have been offered a job, but also alarmed. As a student of European literature, I was ill-qualified to teach high school Chinese. The students were known to be a demanding group, and they had already driven away my predecessor. I was convinced that teaching high school would be asking for trouble and hesitated for a long time, but the summer vacation was approaching and I had no other options. I eventually decided that if the school was offering me a job, I would be so bold as to take up their offer.

So in the autumn of 1934, I became a high school Chinese teacher. I got along well with the principal of the school and with my students, but the other Chinese teachers put me in an uncomfortable position. There were three year groups, four teachers, and twelve classes, and each of us was responsible for teaching three classes. My colleagues were all older than I was. They were experienced, well-trained teachers who barely had to prepare for class. But they each taught three classes in the same year, whereas I taught the remaining class in each year, which required preparing for three separate classes. As a result of my heavy workload and awkward relationship with my colleagues, I was dissatisfied with my job despite earning a fair wage (160 yuan was 3,200 yuan in today's terms). I hadn't achieved my dream of studying abroad, and my "rice bowl" didn't seem secure.

But if the god of fortune exists, he must have been smiling on me: Just as I was beginning to feel trapped, Tsinghua signed an agreement to exchange students with German universities via the German Academic Exchange Service. I was elated, and immediately wrote to apply. When I learned that I had been accepted, I was even happier than I had been when I was accepted to Tsinghua. I would have a bright future; I would never want for anything; and when I returned I would have plenty of job opportunities and a secure job for life.

But there was no escaping the fact that my family was penniless, and I had elderly relatives and a young child to support. I faced another difficult choice. If I turned the offer down, I would be a schoolteacher for the rest of my life and might not even have a secure livelihood. But if I did take the offer, who knew what awaited me? As the poet wrote: "With peach blossoms ahead of me and snow behind me, how dare I turn my horse back now?"

After thinking it over and talking to my family, I decided to go ahead and participate in the exchange program. After all, it was only for two years, and I would be home again before long.

In the summer of 1935, I left for Beijing and Tianjin, where I completed the paperwork necessary for traveling overseas, and took the Trans-Siberian Railway across the Soviet Union to Berlin. It felt as though I were following in the footsteps of the famous Tang dynasty monk Xuanzang, who had long ago journeyed west to bring Buddhist scriptures back to China.

Between graduating from Tsinghua and leaving for Germany, the following image was reflected in my heart's mirror: Chiang was brutally suppressing Communist activity, the Japanese army had invaded, and my fellow students were divided in their allegiances. Those were interesting times.

The peach blossoms ahead of me seemed ethereally beautiful from a distance, but up close they looked like ordinary flowers.

I spent several months in Berlin, which was full of Chinese students, many of whom frittered their time away. Government officials who wanted their children to "study" abroad often sent them to Germany. They despised me, I despised them, and none of us wanted to be so much as seen with the other. Berlin was clearly not for me. In late autumn I left for Göttingen, a university town known for its tradition of scientific excellence. In the seven years I spent living there, I never once left the town.

The German government gave me a monthly stipend of one hundred and twenty marks. Rent alone cost about 40 percent of that, as did food, and I hardly had any money left over. Students funded by the Chinese government had a stipend of eight hundred marks a month, and mine was peanuts compared to theirs. During my years in Germany, I never once took a winter or summer vacation or traveled anywhere, partly because I was penniless and partly because I wanted to make the most of the time I had to study.

After all, I had come all this way to be a student, though I didn't yet have a clear idea of what my studies would focus on. In my first semester, I took Greek with the intention of studying the classics. But I was dismayed to find that I was no match for my German colleagues, many of whom had taken eight years of Latin and six years of Greek in school.

In the spring semester of 1936, I discovered from the course listings that Professor Ernst Waldschmidt would be offering a class on Sanskrit. Mr. Chen Yinke's classes on Buddhism at Tsinghua had awakened my interest in Sanskrit, but there was no way of studying it in China at the time. I was excited by the prospect of studying Sanskrit and immediately decided to take it up. At the time, earning a doctorate at a German university required a major and two minor fields. My major fields were Sanskrit and the Pali language, and my minors were English and Slavic linguistics. I began my formal course of study then.

The term of my scholarship came to an end in 1937, just as full-scale war between China and Japan was sparked by what became known as the Marco Polo Bridge Incident. Japan clearly had its sights on China and all of Asia. Returning home would now be impossible.

Fortunately for me, the chair of the Sinology Department asked me to serve as a lecturer in Chinese, and I immediately agreed. The lectureship was not too time-consuming, and for the rest of my stay in Göttingen, I would spend most of my time studying at the Sanskrit research institute and some of my time lecturing in Sinology.

In 1939, the Second World War broke out. I had thought that a violent war in which millions were to be killed would start with a bang that would terrify the beasts as well as the humans. But war crept up on us silently. The declaration of war was marked only by the barking of a few fascists, and I was already used to that. At the beginning of the war, the Wehrmacht was often successful, but while the Germans were thrilled to hear of the Wehrmacht's victories, every victory was a blow to me. Every time the Wehrmacht won a battle, I would take a sleeping pill at night. I developed a case of chronic insomnia that has stayed with me ever since.

At first, the war had little impact on daily life. Then, gradually, butter and meat were rationed, followed by bread and other necessities. By the time I noticed that the screws were being tightened, they were quite tight indeed. Yet no one complained, apart from a few anti-fascists. The Nazis governed Germany with an iron fist, and the Germans struck me as an enigmatic people.

As the war progressed, Germany was increasingly besieged, and food shortages became acute. I went hungry all day, and at night I dreamed of eating Chinese peanuts. Even in my dreams I am unambitious: Someone else might have dreamed of delicacies like shark's fin or bird's nest, but I dreamed of nothing but peanuts. I felt like a hungry ghost in hell, so hungry I could swallow the planet itself whole.

The war did not interrupt my studies and teaching. At the beginning of the war, there were very few air raids. I finally finished writing my doctoral dissertation. Professor Waldschmidt had been conscripted, and his predecessor, the retired Professor Sieg, stepped in to teach his classes. Professor Sieg was a renowned scholar of Tocharian who had spent decades studying the language. He was old enough to be my grandfather and treated me as his own grandchild. He decided to teach me everything he knew about the Vedas and the grammar of ancient Indian languages. Despite my protestations, he also insisted on teaching me Tocharian. When Professor Waldschmidt was home on furlough, I seized the chance to pass my orals, and also took my Slavic orals with Professor Braun and my English orals with Professor Roeder. Then Professor Sieg continued to advise my work. We met every day. On winter evenings I would walk my octogenarian mentor home along the snow-covered streets. Neither the war nor my constant hunger seemed to matter.

Of course I missed my homeland and family. All communication had been cut off. The poet Tu Fu wrote: "After three months of battle, a letter from home is worth ten thousand pieces of gold." After three years of war, a letter from home would have been worth exponentially more than that to me, except that by then there was no way of getting one through. The lack of news from home only exacerbated my insomnia. I was taking more pills by the day, and my research work was my only solace. By then, British and American air raids had become more frequent, and despite the hunger, I managed to write a few articles between the raids. All the men had been conscripted, and the campus was full of women. Eventually a few men returned, but they were all missing either a leg or an arm, and the chorus of crutches echoing down the hallways became a familiar one.

By now, news of defeat was filtering in from the front lines, and the façade of Nazi lies about the war was beginning to crack. We foreigners could tell that the game was up. There was nothing the Wehrmacht could do to avoid defeat.

My ten years in Germany convinced me that the Germans are among the world's finest peoples. The German civilization has produced more cutting-edge scientific technology, great authors, philosophers, composers, and scientists than any other modern nation. The Germans themselves are honest, upright people, but unfortunately they are also politically naïve, and many of them were genuine supporters of Hitler. Hitler himself frequently insulted the Chinese, whom he saw as destroyers of civilization. That should have made living in Germany harder, but it didn't. I've been told that Chinese people in the United States have difficulty integrating into American society. But in Germany, I lived with German families, and my German classmates, teachers, colleagues, and friends all treated me as one of their own. I never experienced any racism. That, too, was unforgettable.

I never learned how this great nation faced the thought of impending defeat because my German friends seldom discussed the war with me; in the face of extreme privation and brutal air raids, they seemed impassive, perhaps a little lost. Even when the Americans occupied Göttingen in the spring of 1945, and it was clear that fascism had been defeated, the Germans remained unmoved, as if defeat had left them dazed.

Six years of brutal world war had come to an end. Deeply relieved, I immediately thought of my family and of China. I had already been away for ten years, and I could sense the call of the homeland. After some negotiation, the American soldiers occupying Germany agreed to take us to Switzerland in a jeep. I was heartbroken to be saying goodbye to my German teachers and friends, particularly Professor Sieg. He seemed grief-stricken, and his hands were shaking. We both knew we would never see each other again. My eyes brimmed with tears, and I didn't dare look back. My landlady burst into tears at the news. Her husband had died and her son lived far away. We had lived together for years, and once I left Germany, she would be alone again in an empty house. My eyes grew wet as I bid farewell to her and climbed into the jeep. I found myself crafting a poem in the classical style:

After ten years studying in Germany,
My heart desires to return to my homeland.
Instead we cross the border into Switzerland;
Looking back at the trees of the place where I lodged, it begins
    to look like home.

The reflection that these ten years left on my heart's mirror was one of fascist rule, a cruel world war, and my own yearning for home.

We arrived in Switzerland in October 1945. Several months later, in the spring of 1946, we left Switzerland for Marseilles, where we boarded an English steamer taking French troops to Saigon. From Saigon that summer we secured passage via Hong Kong to Shanghai. After eleven years away from China, I was finally home.

By then, Mr. Chen Yinke had recommended me for a post at Peking University, and Messrs. Hu Shi, Fu Sinian, and Tang Yongtong had approved my appointment. I decided that I wasn't going to return to Europe, and wrote to Professor Haloun, an old friend from Göttingen who had moved to Cambridge, to turn down his offer of a job there. I also got in touch with my family and was able to send them some money. I am very grateful to my uncle and aunt and to my wife, Peng Dehua. Without their hard work, our family wouldn't have remained healthy and intact during the eleven years in which I was away.

In China, the raging civil war between the Kuomintang and the Communists made it impossible for me to return home to see my family. Instead, I spent the summer in Shanghai and Nanjing. I was able to visit Mr. Chen Yinke in Nanjing, and meet Mr. Fu Sinian at the Academia Sinica there. In autumn of 1946, I took a boat from Shanghai to Qinhuang Island and then traveled on by train to Beijing. It had been eleven years since I last lived in Beijing and being back was overwhelming. It was a chilly late-autumn day and the streets were full of leaves. Mr. Yin Falu came to pick me up at the station, and he arranged for me to live temporarily in the Red Building, one of the

main buildings on campus. The following day, I met Mr. Tang Yongtong, the dean of the faculty of humanities, who told me that no
Chinese university could appoint scholars returning from overseas to
a post higher than that of associate professor. Mr. Fu Sinian had told
me the same thing in Nanjing. Of course I would have been content
with any post at Peking University, and I wasn't going to ask for
more. But after just over a week, Mr. Tang informed me that I had
been appointed a full professor and chair of the Eastern Languages
Department. I was thirty-five. I had probably set the record for the
fastest promotion to full professor. This was more than I could have
hoped for. I was determined to work hard and publish industriously
so as not to let down the teachers and elders who believed in me
enough to give me this opportunity.

At this time the political situation was very unstable. Chiang Kai-
shek's Kuomintang had dropped all pretense of good governance and
was showing its true colors. Corrupt tax officials lined their own
pockets, buying houses, cars, and mistresses. Currency inflation was
rampant, and even a professor could barely eke out a living. Your
paycheck would begin to lose its value within hours after you received it. We all converted our pay immediately into silver or American dollars, and only converted it back into Chinese currency just
before spending it. Feeling the weight of a handful of coins in my
palm always gave me a sense of security.

The students themselves were bitterly divided. The Kuomintang
was struggling, and the Communist students were pressing their advantage fiercely. It was said that there were two places in Beijing that
had already been liberated by the Communists: the Democracy
Square of Peking University, and the Tsinghua campus. Where I lived,
in the Red Building on the old campus, we were sometimes threatened by gangs of thugs in the employ of the Kuomintang. At night,
we would board up the area with tables and chairs against the invaders. This was unbearable but also quite absurd.

It is a natural law that an organism rotting from within will eventually die. In the spring of 1949, Beijing was finally liberated.

During those three years, the reflection on my heart's mirror was of darkness before the break of dawn.

I often conceive of my life as being divided into two halves, the first consisting of the thirty-eight years in which I lived in the old China, and the second consisting of the unknown number of years in which I will have lived in the new China—since I have no intention of dying soon, I don't yet know exactly how many years that will be.

I describe 1949 as a personal turning point for me because there was such a great difference between living under Kuomintang and Communist rule. Like many of the older intellectuals who had not fled overseas or retreated with the Kuomintang to Taiwan, I knew very little about the Communists and wasn't attracted to Communism. But our experience of the Kuomintang made us enthusiastic in welcoming the People's Liberation Army into Beijing. In the early years of Communist rule, the new government was energetic and untainted by corruption, and its policies were popular with the masses. Much of the dirt of the old society was wrung out and washed away. We all had high hopes for a prosperous new society.

It took us some time to adjust to the Communists' new practices. I don't know how other older intellectuals felt, but I was forty at the time, in early middle age, and balked at Communist ways. At political rallies, the cries of "Long live..." stuck in my throat. It even took me a while to get used to wearing a modern Mao suit instead of traditional Chinese dress.

But before long, I was a changed person. I got used to the new way of doing things. The skies seemed bluer and the grass greener, with flowers blooming everywhere. I felt ten years younger, and I had endless faith in the future of the Chinese people. At meetings and rallies, I shouted slogans as loudly and passionately as anyone else. In retrospect, that was the happiest time of my life.

Yet I was ashamed to think that I was enjoying the fruits of my fellow countrymen's labor and sacrifice without having contributed anything myself. The Chinese people finally had a society we could be proud of, and I had done nothing to help achieve it. It was true that I hadn't joined the Kuomintang or capitulated to German fascists. But while other young people my age were fighting and dying for a new society, I had been pursuing my own ambitions in distant Germany. There could be nothing more despicable than this. Even my so-called scholarly learning was abhorrent to me.

I was convinced of my own guilt and, by extension, of the guilt of intellectuals as a class. This almost Christian feeling of guilt remained with me for many years.

I fantasized about turning the clock back and having a chance to prove myself in the war. I knew I would have been willing to sacrifice my life for my country and for the revolution. I even imagined that I would have volunteered to die protecting the Great Leader, if given the chance.

In my self-hatred, I worshipped three kinds of people: old cadres, soldiers, and workers. They were perfect, and I would never catch up even if I spent the rest of my life trying to emulate them.

My deep-seated belief in my own guilt made me ready to root out the capitalist impulses in my own thinking and to adopt the proletariat mind-set (even though I still can't say what that mind-set entails, apart from being selfless). In any case, I was prepared to remake myself in the image required by the new society. Thirty eventful years have passed since then.

The first great political campaigns after Liberation were the Three-Antis, Five-Antis, and Thought Reform Campaigns. I participated in them all as a sincere believer. I had never been corrupt, so the Three-Antis and Five-Antis Campaigns didn't affect me. But I myself believed that I urgently needed to reform my capitalist thinking. First, before Liberation my experience of the Kuomintang had led me to assume that politics was always dirty and to want nothing to do with it; second, I used to believe that Outer Mongolia had been stolen from China by the Soviet Union, and that the Chinese Communist Party was under Soviet control. I denounced these two former beliefs of mine in thought reform meetings. At the time, there were small, medium, and large "tubs," venues of different sizes for public self-criticism. As the department chair, I was required to "bathe in a medium-size tub," or make a speech at a department meeting. Fortunately, since my speech did not arouse the anger of the masses, I wasn't required to self-criticize at a meeting of all students.

Even the water in the medium-size tub was hot enough as it was. Debate was heated, some of it sincere and the rest less so. I had never experienced anything like it in my life. Each comment felt like an arrow aimed straight at me. But because my sense of my own guilt was so strong, I almost enjoyed the experience of being criticized. It made me break out in a sweat like in a Turkish hot bath. When the assembly finally allowed me to pass, I was so moved that I wept, feeling cleansed of my capitalist thinking.

There were many true believers like myself, but there were also others whose sole aim was to pass. One particular professor had bathed countless times in small- and medium-size tubs, but the masses had never voted to let him pass, and he eventually graduated to the big tub. He must have made up his mind to pass once and for all. He made a stirring speech, abusing both himself and his capitalist father and mother. The crowds were touched. But then the chair of that meeting noticed that he had noted "Cry here!" in red ink at several places in his notes and would begin sobbing at those predetermined points. As soon as the chair announced this to the crowd, it caused a great stir. Needless to say, he didn't pass.

We criticized the movie *The Life of Wu Xun* for depicting the Qing dynasty educational reformer whom the Communists considered bourgeois. Then we criticized the movie *Spring in February* for glorifying bourgeois romance. We criticized Hu Shi and Hu Pingbo, as well as Hu Feng's "counterrevolutionary conspiracy," Hu Feng being defined as an enemy of socialism. Many other prominent figures in the art and academic worlds were enmeshed in the campaign against Hu Feng. The campaigns began to dig up its victims' counterrevolutionary histories, and several of them committed suicide. One driver at Peking University told me that he was extra careful whenever he drove at night, because at any moment someone might leap out of the shadows and throw themselves under the wheels.

The political campaigns reached their first climax in 1957. That year's campaigns were larger, more threatening, and more extensive than any previous campaigns.

At first we were told this was simply an Internal Party campaign in which everyone was invited to voice their opinions: "Nothing you know isn't worth saying, and nothing you say isn't worth saying in full" was the slogan. People still believed unquestioningly in the Party, and many naïvely loyal people voiced their criticism. Some of them were soon categorized as "rightists." It was proclaimed that rightism was "a form of enemy conflict treated as a form of internal conflict," and that rightists would never be rehabilitated.

Some of the rightists pointed out that this conspiracy against them was unfair, that they had been promised the freedom to voice their opinions without being attacked. The official answer came from Chairman Mao himself: Yes, this is indeed a conspiracy, but it is a conspiracy in broad daylight! Many rightists were denounced, though not persecuted as "enemies of the people," and several had grown old by the time they were rehabilitated twenty years later. Nonetheless, their rehabilitation demonstrates that the Party is both strong enough and confident enough to admit its mistakes.

I don't know how many people were wrongly categorized as rightists at the time. Apparently there was a quota, and a given number of people had to be declared rightists in order to meet it. In some cases, this was utterly absurd. I began to realize that this campaign, like so many others, was an excuse to persecute intellectuals. But even so, I supported it out of my own sense of guilt.

In 1958, the Anti-Rightist Movement drew to a close. But the masses' tremendous momentum was immediately plowed into a new push to liberate the factors of production and eradicate capitalist thinking. Capitalist thinking was to be eradicated in an operation called Uprooting White Flags, which would replace university professors and members of the Chinese Academy of Sciences who were considered backward, capitalist, and "white" with revolutionary, forward-thinking "red flags."

The liberation of factors of production took the form of smelting steel in backyard furnaces. This was a disaster. There's nothing wrong with collecting scrap iron and melting it down. But when people ran out of scrap metal, they began to melt down useful objects like cooking pots. The proliferation of tiny furnaces all over China must have been visible from space, like so many stars. All they produced were useless lumps of pig iron. As for the people's commune, it was considered an innovation in both production and ideology. The slogan of the time was: "If Communism is heaven, the people's commune is a bridge to heaven."

Everyone wants to get to heaven, and people's communes spread like wildfire across the country. That year's harvest happened to be good, and people ate their fill. Stoves in private homes fell into disuse as everyone ate in the mess halls. Grain rotted in the fields because no one went out to reap. The power of the masses had been overestimated, as had the power of human beings to conquer nature. Sparrows had been defined as one of the four pests, and people bent all their energies toward destroying sparrow nests and shooting sparrows down.[1] Production figures were also exaggerated to incredible proportions: Fields that had previously produced several hundred pounds of grain were now said to be producing tens of thousands of pounds. For that to have been the case, the fields would have had to be carpeted in a thick layer of grain.

I was about forty-seven years old at the time. I was a grown man, college educated, and had even studied abroad—yet I believed every last word of the agricultural reports. In the words of the slogan, I believed that "the fields are as fertile as the farmers are bold." I despised skeptics whose minds had not yet been liberated, now that I was more Marxist and more revolutionary than they were.

Three years of famine followed. It's clear in retrospect that the Great Famine wasn't primarily a natural disaster and that the suffering was worsened by human error. In any case, the whole country starved. Having already survived five years of hunger in Germany, I was an old hand at hunger and didn't have any complaints.

The country had clearly taken an overly leftist turn, and the task at hand was to correct excessive leftism. That was apparently what the central government originally planned to do. But then at the Lushan Conference, Peng Dehuai wrote Mao a private letter full of forthright criticism. Little did he know that this would swing the Party's focus from anti-leftism to anti-rightism. Peng's letter was widely circulated, and he was accused of forming a clique of Party opponents and ostracized. To this day, of all the Communist pioneers who contributed to liberating China, I have the greatest respect for General Peng, a courageous man whose willingness to speak up was an instance of characteristically Chinese integrity.

Since we had been directed to oppose the rightists, we did. After more than a decade of continuous political struggle, the intellectuals knew the drill. We all took turns persecuting each other. This went on until the Socialist Education Movement, which, in my view, was a precursor to the Cultural Revolution. I will now discuss those two movements.

Peking University was one of the earliest sites of the Socialist Education Movement. It split the school into two camps: the persecutors and the persecuted. Without quite knowing what I was doing, I joined the ranks of the persecutors. For the first time since Liberation, I began to question the Party. The Communists asserted that "the intellectuals were in power," even though the university administration was clearly run by experienced Party cadres rather than professors. I couldn't help wondering why Party leaders kept repeating that slogan when it was obviously wrong.

Eventually the Municipal Party Committee intervened in the movement on campus, rehabilitating the university administrators who had been denounced at the International Hotel Conference. This would eventually become the impetus for the Cultural Revolution.

In the autumn of 1965, after the International Hotel Conference, I was sent to Nankou Village in the suburbs of Beijing, to help take the Socialist Education Movement out to the villages. Here the intellectuals were in power. We were given all financial, administrative, and Party authority. We were also subject to strict rules: We were not permitted to cook for ourselves, we would eat on a rotation in the village, and we were not allowed meat, fish, or eggs. It was forbidden to mention your title or salary. Since the villagers were mostly making thirty or forty cents a day, whereas I was on a salary of four or five hundred a month, we thought they would be stunned if they realized how much we made. Nowadays, we wouldn't tell villagers how much we are paid because they would only laugh at us. How the times have changed!

In the winter of 1965, Yao Wenyuan's essay "On the New Historical Play *Hai Rui Dismissed from Office*" signaled the beginning of the Cultural Revolution. I said openly in Nankou that I knew all three co-authors of the controversial column "Notes from a Three-Family Village." One of my students became known during the Cultural Revolution for odd behavior such as signing political banners with his own name. He remembered these words, and would later use them as evidence to label me "a hanger-on of the Three-Family Village."

On June 4, 1966, I was summoned back to campus to take part in the Cultural Revolution, the first stage of which consisted in persecuting "capitalist academic authorities." This movement was clearly an excuse to molest the intellectuals, and I was one of its targets. I might have admitted to being a capitalist, though I wouldn't dare call myself an academic authority. But somehow the masses left me alone.

A revolutionary committee was later established at Peking University, headed by the author of the first Marxist-Leninist big-character poster. This woman had powerful backing. It was said that she even had a direct line to heaven and was a close associate of Jiang Qing. She was an ignorant person who often made mistakes when she spoke, but that didn't stop her from being imperious and arrogant. Now she was famous, and tens of thousands of tourists flocked to Peking University every day, like the legendary monks who had journeyed to India in search of Buddhist scriptures. The campus was in chaos.

As the movement developed, Peking University split into different factions. The one backed by this woman, the Empress Dowager, had the upper hand. It was called the New Peking University Commune, or New Beida, and it was able to bully its opponent, Jinggangshan. But both groups were equally unruly, beating their victims up, stealing, and destroying things. The authorities had decreed "There is no crime in revolution, it is reasonable to revolt!" That was the only law these students recognized.

Having survived the first wave of storms, I remained happily neutral for some time. If I had stayed out of the fray, I would probably have been safe. I was in the position of the legendary general Wu Zixu: I had escaped past Zhaoguan, the last pass before the state of Wu, to safety. But although I am normally a fainthearted, cowardly person, I decided to do something abnormally bold. Only on very few occasions over the course of my lifetime have I been so bold, and now that I think back to these abnormal occasions, I consider them the best things I have ever done.

The Cultural Revolution was one such occasion. While the Empress Dowager was exploiting her political connections to do whatever she wanted, the movement on campus became increasingly violent and savage. The Red Guards were raiding homes, beating up and screaming at their victims, hanging wooden boards around their necks and putting tall hats on their heads, humiliating them, spreading false rumors about them, and in some cases murdering them. In my opinion, their brutality contravened the revolutionary people's line. I knowingly chose to risk my position of relative safety by joining the fray. In my diary, I wrote that "I would die to protect the direction of the Great Leader's revolution!" These words were heartfelt.

I was also confident that I had no flaws or secrets in my past that could be used against me. I had never belonged to the Kuomintang or any other counterrevolutionary organization, and I had never been on the side of the landowners and capitalists. I was risking my neck, but I thought I might survive unharmed. I made a deliberate choice to openly defy the Empress Dowager.

Little did I know—or perhaps deep down, I did know—that this choice would land me in the cowshed. I had some influence among the students, and the Empress Dowager was furious to learn that I opposed her. She would not rest until I was defeated. My house was raided, and I was struggled against, beaten up, and bruised all over. When humiliated, I'm not the sort of person who can just let things go. I was so devastated by the struggle sessions that I decided to commit suicide. Once I had made the decision, I became extraordinarily calm. I put a stash of sleeping pills and medicines in my pocket, and took one last look at my aunt and wife, who had suffered alongside me. I was about to step out the door, climb over the wall, and escape, when there was a violent knocking at the door, and New Beida's Red Guards came to escort me to the cafeteria for another struggle session.

I had had the narrowest of escapes! This struggle session was exceptionally violent, and I was punched and kicked so savagely I could barely get up. But it made me realize that the human capacity to endure pain is limitless. I decided that I would survive. I would not die—I would live.

I did survive, but by the time I left the cowshed, I had become little better than an idiot. When I walked into a shop to buy something, I didn't know what to say. I was used to staring at the ground wherever I went and being cursed and threatened. I stuttered and hesitated whenever I saw people—I barely felt human. I belonged to the walking dead.

I did survive, but I couldn't help wondering why I had forgotten the saying "The scholar can be killed, but he cannot be humiliated." Since I had had the courage to speak up, why had I not had the courage to protest my indignities by ending my life? I sometimes felt that having chosen to live was shameful. Even more strangely, I never opposed or resented the Cultural Revolution itself until the Gang of Four was toppled in 1976. Until then, I had supported the state of continuous revolution that plagued the country and failed to associate my own suffering with it. As you can tell, I am not a political animal.

I spent forty years worshipping cadres, soldiers, and workers, as I mentioned above, and feeling guilty about my own vocation. Everything sacred to me was destroyed by the Cultural Revolution. It is true that I still respect these three types of people. But as for the Cultural Revolution itself, which I used to support wholeheartedly, I now consider it an unprecedentedly violent, ignorant, farcical tragedy, an unforgettable disgrace to the Chinese people.

After the Gang of Four was toppled and the Cultural Revolution ended, the authorities instituted an economic policy of reform and opening up. It has gained widespread support and become very successful within only a few years. All of China, and all the intellectuals, are hopeful about the future.

This has been my experience of the forty or so years since Liberation. During this time, my heart's mirror reflected campaign after campaign after campaign, including the experience of political campaigns that I shared with many other intellectuals. It reflected my own journey from blindly supporting the campaigns to thinking more clearheadedly and the progress that China has made from the brink of economic and political disaster to relative prosperity.

I have lived through more than eighty years of the twentieth century, and in seven years' time, this century and this millennium will be at an end. These have been interesting, changing times, and the reflections in my mirror have been colorful and full of variation, reflecting both narrow bridges and well-lit roads. I cannot promise that my mirror is absolutely free of error. But its reflections are accurate and reliable.

I have held this mirror for eighty years. In retrospect, how would I judge its record of the twentieth century and of my own life? As the poet wrote: "Now that I know what sorrow tastes like, I would speak of it but have no words. Instead I say: What a chilly autumn day!" I say: What a chilly winter day!

There is only one thing of which I am certain: The twenty-first century will be the century in which the culture at the heart of Eastern civilization, Chinese culture, experiences a renaissance. Today's most pressing questions of human survival, such as the explosion in population growth, environmental pollution, habitat destruction, the holes in the ozone layer, the limits of industrial food production, and the limited freshwater supply, can only be addressed by the Chinese civilization. This is my firm and final belief.

*February 17, 1993*

# Notes

AUTHOR'S PREFACE

1    The recurring motif of people who "eat" other people is a reference to one of the seminal texts of the May Fourth Movement, Lu Xun's 1918 short story "A Madman's Diary" ("Kuang ren ri ji").

2    The Empress Dowager was a nickname for Nie Yuanzi (b. 1921), a philosophy professor and instigator of the turmoil on campus at the start of the Cultural Revolution, and an allusion to the Empress Dowager Cixi (1835–1908) who controlled the Qing dynasty's imperial court for half a century.

3    Scar literature is the name given to a genre of Chinese literature that emerged in the late 1970s, depicting the experiences of their authors during the Cultural Revolution.

THE SOCIALIST EDUCATION MOVEMENT

1    As part of the Socialist Education Movement, conceived to persuade peasants of the benefits of collectivism and the communes, intellectuals were also sent to the countryside to help with agricultural work.

2    Wu Han was a leading historian who had earlier called on Party cadres to emulate the outspoken Ming dynasty official Hai Rui. A play he wrote for a Beijing Opera company, *Hai Rui Dismissed from Office*, won Mao's approval when it was performed in 1961, but Jiang Qing

argued that it was, in fact, an attack on Mao's policies, a veiled critique of the dishonest reporting of agricultural output. Mao personally revised the junior propagandist Yao Wenyuan's polemic against Wu Han's play. Yao would later be known as one of the Gang of Four.

3    The Communist Revolution of 1949 is customarily referred to as Liberation.

4    "Notes from a Three-Family Village" was a weekly column commissioned by a Party-run magazine. The three ill-fated authors of the column, Wu Han, Deng Tuo, and Liao Mosha, were all persecuted in the Cultural Revolution; Deng Tuo would later commit suicide and Wu Han would die in prison.

## JUNE FOURTH, 1966

1    The May 16th Notification was a classified document containing denunciations of Peng Zhen and others, and recording the politburo's approval of the Cultural Revolution.

2    This is a poem that Ji wrote in his diary upon leaving Germany after more than a decade in Göttingen.

3    The airplane position was a stress position often used by Red Guards, in which the victim was made to bend over at the waist with arms stretched out or bent backward.

## CHOOSING A LABEL THAT FIT

1    Qi Baishi (1864–1957) and Wang Xuetao (1903–1982) were both influential Chinese brush painters.

2    At criticism meetings, individuals who had committed "thought errors" would be invited to participate in public self-criticism and be open to verbal attacks.

## JOINING THE FRAY

1    Hu Shi (1891–1962) was a prominent intellectual and cultural reformer influential in the May Fourth Movement.

2   "Going it alone" was the phrase used to refer to individual peasants who refused to join a village commune and preferred to farm on their own.

## REFORM THROUGH LABOR BEGINS

1   Cross talk is a traditional art form consisting of a richly allusive, punning dialogue between two performers.

## THE GREAT STRUGGLE SESSION

1   *The Water Margin* is a fourteenth-century novel recording the exploits of a band of outlaws gathered at Mount Liang.

## IN THE COWSHED (1)

1   Hu Feng (1902–1985) was a prominent literary theorist who became the target of a national criticism campaign.

2   Ji refers to an incident in which Emperor Yongzheng (1678–1735) seized on a minor linguistic flourish in a memorial submitted by General Nian Gengyao (1679–1726) as an excuse to execute him.

3   Yuan Shikai (1859–1916) was a Qing dynasty general who staged a brief military coup in 1916, declaring himself president of the newly established Republic of China; the coup lasted only eighty-three days.

## IN THE COWSHED (2)

1   The Dunhuang manuscripts consist of important religious and secular documents discovered in the Mogao Caves in western China and dating back as far as the fifth century.

## HALF LIBERATED

1   The *erhu* is a two-stringed bowed musical instrument believed to have originated in central Asia.

## FURTHER REFLECTIONS

1   This "old revolutionary" was Zhou Yang (1908–1989), a controversial character who took the lead in several political campaigns, including

the campaign against Hu Feng that Ji mentions later. Zhou was imprisoned at the beginning of the Cultural Revolution and not released until 1978.

2   *The Scholars* is a 1750 novel by Wu Jingzi satirizing the civil service examination system that produced imperial China's scholar bureaucrats.

3   The campaigns, which took place in 1951 and 1952, targeted corruption and bureaucratic wastefulness.

4   Wu Xun (1838–1896) was a late Qing dynasty figure who rose from poverty to become a landlord and used his money to establish schools for the very poor. Redology is the study of the eighteenth-century classic novel *Dream of the Red Chamber* by Cao Xueqin. Hu Shi (1891–1962) was a historian and leading reformer of the May Fourth Movement.

5   This is a recasting of the first line of the poem "Climbing a Tower" ("Deng Lou") by the Tang dynasty poet Du Fu (717–770): "The traveler climbing a tall tower to gaze at flowers is overwhelmed by grief." (See "The Great Struggle Session.") Du Fu's poem condemned the weak central government during a time of political turmoil.

APPENDIX: MY HEART IS A MIRROR

1   The four pests to be exterminated were rats, flies, mosquitoes, and sparrows.

JI XIANLIN (1911–2009) was born in the impoverished flatlands of Shandong Province, only weeks before the Qing government was overthrown, and educated in Germany in the 1930s. After the Second World War, he returned to China to co-chair the Eastern Languages Department at Peking University. A distinguished scholar of Sanskrit and Pali, Ji was best known as an influential essayist and public intellectual. The former Chinese premier Wen Jiabao paid visits to the author during his final years and made it known that he considered Ji a mentor.

ZHA JIANYING is a journalist and nonfiction writer. She is the author of two books in English, *China Pop: How Soap Operas, Tabloids, and Bestsellers Are Transforming a Culture* and *Tide Players: The Movers and Shakers of a Rising China*. Her work has appeared in a variety of publications, including *The New Yorker, The New York Times*, and *Dushu*. She divides her time between Beijing and New York City.

CHENXIN JIANG was born in Singapore and grew up in Hong Kong. Recent and forthcoming translations include a novel by Xiao Bai for HarperCollins and one by Zsuzsanna Gahse for Dalkey Archive Press. She received the 2011 Susan Sontag Prize for Translation, as well as a PEN Translation Grant for her work on Ji Xianlin. Chenxin also translates from Italian and German. She studied comparative literature and creative writing at Princeton University.